The

Unconverted Missionary

Matthew McNeil

For Krys, Josie and Jessica.
My three treasures.

Preface

Perhaps you're reading this because the title got your attention.

Although I am converted to Christ I wasn't fully embracing some of His harder teachings—one in particular—and it took a deeper conversion experience to finally recognize it alone is essential to what Christ asks of us, which I share toward the end of the book.

A fellow missionary made a comment to me after serving on the field for several years. "I feel like I've been dropped into a mortar and pestle, and God is delighting in crushing me, grinding me to powder." Another missionary wrote, "I've never cried more, cussed more, been more frustrated and angry, and feeling so incompetent than I have as a missionary."

After 25 years of serving on the mission field, I've discovered that God brings missionaries to a point of deeper conversion through a process of crushing for a purpose—to learn the value of following Him with a limp; and with that disability we are better positioned to bear more fruit. I decided to weave my "deeper conversion experience" into an autobiography, not because my story is so important, but rather as an honest chronicle of my journey.

Some authors write like some musicians play music; their gift flows from them naturally. I can hammer away at writing a single paragraph for three hours lacking anything flowing or natural, which leaves me frustrated and wearied. Several years ago, I read a Christian book that was choppy and disjointed. Someone referred to the author's sentences as "inelegant," and there was "no cohesive flow" to his storyline at all, but it became a national best seller. I thought if I ever wrote a book, I'd write it in a similar style; perhaps not as disjointed, but certainly lacking the flow of a gifted writer. Low personal expectations, I guess, is what finally enabled me to give this a try—although having no pretenses it might be a best seller.

I hope that by reading my story, you might see a thread woven throughout my narrative that we all share in common—searching for a story that counts for something. It will take you far less time to read my story than it took me to live it, but I hope you enjoy the journey.

CONTENTS

And the Lord said,
"Simon…when you are converted, strengthen your brothers."

Introduction

I instructed one of the short-term visitors from our home church to follow me down a narrow mud-caked trail which led to a shallow creek at the bottom of a ravine, about two hundred feet below the area where our new building would be. We had staked out reference points for the construction site in a clearing located in the center of a mountain village (*sitio*) where a group of native aboriginal families had been relocated following the 1991 eruption of Mt. Pinatubo two years earlier, which had destroyed their homes and livelihood.

The village was situated on an open ridge adjacent to a dense overgrown jungle where the Bataan lowlands rise up to converge with the base of Mt. Mariveles, a dormant volcano sitting quietly at the southernmost tip the Zambales mountain range. The view from every hut faced east, overlooking the expansive valley floor below with a panoramic view of rice paddies, farm land, fish ponds and a few small towns. Behind the village almost within an arrow's flight stood the mountain itself; a massive intimidating presence standing like a protective sentinel keeping watch over the people. The South China Sea, also known as the West Philippine Sea, sits on the opposite side of the range. Directly north was Lingayen Gulf where U.S. and Allied forces landed on the lengthy beachhead in 1945 as part of General Douglas MacArthur's promise to return and retake the Philippines from the Japanese invaders who had brought death and oppression to the islands.

We had the privilege of being introduced to the villagers the previous year and prayerfully determined the need to educate the children was a priority as we considered a long-term community development assistance effort. The building was intended to be a multi-purpose facility which would serve as the schoolhouse, community center, and hopefully a church if our evangelism and discipleship efforts were fruitful. The construction plans were simple enough and the informal architectural drawing was sketched on a sheet of notebook paper. The floor would be a reinforced four-inch thick concrete slab. Waist high stub walls fashioned from handmade cement hollow blocks, formed with metal lined wooden molds, would be affixed along the outward edge of the slab and solidified by filling in the hollow spaces with concrete mortar. Wood framing would then be attached to the top of the stub walls, rising high enough to complete the necessary ceiling height. Four corner posts with two additional load bearing columns placed at the center along the perimeter would support the trusses and corrugated sheet metal (*yero*) that would make up the roof.

The basic components of concrete are cement, sand and gravel aggregate, and water. We planned to use shovels to mix everything together on thick plastic sheeting laid out on the bare ground. I had hand mixed concrete before and it's back-breaking work that will exhaust a grown man in a matter of minutes if he's not used to it. Unfortunately, a significant logistical problem and one enigmatic cultural dilemma presented some challenges. As it turned out, the only water source was at the bottom of that ravine and surprisingly, for some reason we could not understand, none of the men in the village offered to assist us with the project. Specifically, they refused to help us haul water for the concrete mix. This was a bit frustrating because our goal was to help their children get a formal education, and a small school building was necessary for the teachers who had committed to travelling up into the village every week from the lowlands.

Every round trip down the ravine then hiking back up while hauling a plastic five-gallon Jerry can water container required us to pass by the village men standing near the trail head tying *cogan* grass together into sheaves. They acted entirely indifferent as they watched us struggle to carry water up that long trail in the overwhelming tropical heat and heavy humidity, which felt like a warm wet blanket draped over our shoulders. The village women sat to the side under the shade of a tree, watching us as if they were monitoring our laborious progress.

I generally default to the value of equal sharing, especially if the benefit tends to favor the other person more than myself. In this case, we weren't building the school to benefit me, so there was no reason the men of the village couldn't help us pack in the water. On the third trip up the hill, drenched in sweat and struggling to catch my breath, I turned to my visitor and said, "I'm going to do something but I don't know what's going to happen, so just stand there and don't move." His eyes grew larger after hearing this, and a look of worried confusion spread across his face.

What I did next sent a very clear message, which I'm quite sure transcended all cultural barriers of every tribal group in the world, that didn't need to be interpreted or explained by a seasoned anthropologist.

I hollered at the men standing about 30 feet from us in order to get their attention. As they faced me with a curious look, I unscrewed the cap from the heavy container filled with water I had just lugged up the hill and proceeded to pour out the entire contents on the ground in front of them. Then, for added dramatic effect that helped sensationalize my point, I vigorously shook out the extra drops before throwing the empty container at their feet—an act I fully intended to serve as an indictment against them.

* * *

Have you ever been in a situation where the perception of time seems to slow down? The nanosecond that container can left my hand on the trajectory I'd sent it, I thought to myself that perhaps I misjudged my choice of self-expression as I watched it arc through the air in slow motion away from me. As much as I willed for it to happen, that container would not return to my hand once it left my grasp. It was committed. I think my friend thought I'd lost my mind by blatantly confronting this group of tribal men in that particular manner; in front of their womenfolk who were sitting nearby with wide eyes, gazing with rapt attention as they watched this crazy foreigner single handedly confront a group of men—their men, in their own village. I heard my friend silently gasp, and I'm fairly certain he thought it would be our last day on the planet.

I imagine that seasoned missionaries who'd spent years working in remote villages would have advised against my rash action. I recalled as a kid, watching a cartoon show where *Bugs Bunny* was about to be cooked in a large pot over an open fire. I had no idea what to expect and prepared myself for the worst. Either I'd be cooked like *Bugs,* slow roasted like one of the wild pigs they'd hunted and suspended from a bamboo stake over a bed of red hot coals, tattooed on my backside with a tribal icon that would never be viewed as cultural art, or I would be led to the edge of the village and told in their own way that I was never to return.

Time stood still for a moment and I could tell by everyone's facial expression that a brief mental disconnect just happened while they attempted to process what I had just done. The village men were shocked, the women were astounded, and I was planning my escape. The guy from my home church was entirely on his own.

What happened next was something I could never have anticipated, even if it followed a script written for the lead actors in a movie.

Between the Equator and the North Pole

I grew up halfway between the Equator and the North Pole. At least that's what it said on the road sign located a handful of miles from my parent's home in eastern Oregon alongside Interstate 84, where I spent most of my childhood. For many years, I thought that green sign marked a distinct significance about where we lived that made it special—kind of like having a publicly showcased honorable-mention ribbon you might win at the county fair, which the local townsfolk could lay claim to. It actually said *45th PARALLEL – HALF WAY BETWEEN THE EQUATOR AND NORTH POLE.*

In the mind of a young boy, that sign was intriguing as it stood there silently pointing to far off places like the *Equator* where Pollywog sailors are ceremoniously initiated—based on ancient nautical tradition—into the realm of King Neptune and his court as they cross that invisible demarcation line on masted schooners and return as Shellbacks. Or the *North Pole,* where Robert Peary teamed with Inuits and sled dogs to fight Jack Frost and deep glacial crevasses in his icy quest to become the first man to reach the northernmost point on the earth. That simple sign was a landmark, standing there proudly announcing something beyond itself, like the lamp-post in C.S. Lewis' chronicles that marked the border between our world and the imaginary land of Narnia—which caused Lucy Pevensie to exclaim, "It will not go out of my mind that if we pass this post and lantern, either we shall find strange adventures or else some great changes of our fortunes."

I later discovered that sign wasn't necessarily highlighting a prominent point of distinction, indicating something noteworthy we alone could claim. Instead, I learned that the 45th Parallel is a theoretical line stretching across the entire globe that practically bisects France and passes through another dozen countries. Copies of our sign and other markers stating the same thing are scattered around the world. A street in Stavropol Russia is actually named *45th Parallel Street,* and there's an obelisk erected in the center of the Piazza Statuto marking where it passes through Turin, Italy.

During most of my childhood, just as that simple green sign stated, I always felt like I lived half-way between something and somewhere else.

* * *

Some moments from our childhood are forever embedded in our souls. They become so much a part of the intimate narratives of our lives that even when shared with others, they can never be truly understood with the same depth of emotions we felt as we lived them. If the memories I collected as a small boy could be likened to my prized shiny metal Steelies and cats-eyed Aggie marbles that I treasured and protected in my small leather drawstring pouch; the ones I cherished above all others were the memories I kept when we lived in a small town of Bonners Ferry in the northern panhandle of Idaho, about 15 miles south of the US-Canadian border. In the center of town and across a side street from the two-story red-brick federal post office was the Sears and Roebuck catalog store my dad managed. It was actually a walk-in mail order store, which were quite common in rural America during the mid-20th century until the late 1970s. Inventory was sparse, with a stove and a stack of popular radial car tires taking up space in one corner of the store while a few various household items sat on shelves in an adjacent corner.

The focal point was the long retail counter where thick Sears catalogs sat open for people to browse through. People could order things like a new blouse, a pair of jeans, a hand mixer, socket wrenches, a sewing machine, or choose amongst countless other items pictured in the full-colored pages. Once ordered, items were shipped from the nearest distribution center and delivered to the store after a week or two. It was a relatively efficient system and people were satisfied with the fact they didn't need to physically handle or inspect the merchandise before placing their order.

My parents rented a small three-bedroom house located at the top of the southern hill in a neighborhood adorned with maple and chestnut trees that stood as silent watchmen over a sprawling playground covering several blocks—where dreams came to life in the eyes of young boys with expansive imaginations. Our neighborhood and that small town was for the most part the extent of my worldview.

Every newly embarked adventure felt untamed as a young boy, whether it was digging a hole to China between the apple trees in the backyard, fashioning peashooters from Mom's wooden clothespins, collecting shiny auburn colored conkers from under the green boughs of chestnut trees, scooping up tadpoles into glass Mason jars from the creek that ran through a nearby gully, catching garter snakes, or making battleships from cardboard boxes.

I remember catching my first rainbow trout in Blue Lake and holding it in my hands as the sun glistened off its slimy scales, building a go-cart from a kit to race down Stone's Hill, and learning to ride a bicycle with no hands.

A married couple with two young kids lived across the street and I remember watching in amazement as they trained for competitive lumberjack shows by practicing Jack-n-Jill bucksaw cutting, axe throwing, and speed chopping through logs. The man was a logger and their backyard looked like a makeshift lumber yard where he deposited scrap logs gathered from the local sawmill. After each practice, he would set his 6' long crosscut saws up on a makeshift rack in the driveway and skillfully sharpen the serrated teeth in preparation for their next practice session or an actual logging event. I still recall the smell of fresh sawdust and chain oil that lubricated the saws to cut through thick logs with fluid precision.

We played cowboys and Indians, retold local myths and stories, and formed unguarded friendships. We also built tree forts, learned how to handle slingshots, trapped squirrels, and made bows and arrows from willow branches. On a dare, a friend and I would venture out on dangerous treks and hike down to the train tracks where we laid nickels on the shiny steel rails just as a train was rapidly approaching. We hid in the thickets as we watched the enormous BNSF diesel locomotives speed past, carrying their long serpentine line of cars. Once the caboose had passed indicating it was safe, we ran out to retrieve our nickels which were flattened beyond recognition and devoid of any markings. Every night, as the small nightlight cast its assuring glow, I was content to fall asleep feeling that each day had been adventurous and fulfilling.

* * *

The combination of all these experiences were my *eternal summer*, as Mark Twain wrote. However, I also did some dumb things during those years which ended up costing me. For example, I can honestly say that I don't know why I used my *Old Timer* pocketknife to cut through Dad's new garden hose, which I'm sure was probably from Sears. If I recall correctly, I was just checking to see if it was sharp. That cost me a good spanking. Another mistake became family folklore and the story is often referenced as a classic tale woven amongst our tapestry of collected sibling experiences, as it is constantly retold during family gatherings. It involved the time Dad took my new bicycle away from me when I was about six years old. He had bought my younger brother, Scott, and I identical Schwinn Stingrays with the banana seat, chrome fenders, and "ape hanger" handlebars. They were high definition, metal flaked, candy-color-purple "wheelie" dream machines that were envied by every other kid on the block. Today they're called classics and a restored original can command several hundred dollars.

I remember being so overwhelmed upon receiving this beautiful bike that I forgot a basic rule of gratitude I never forgot again after the hard lesson my dad taught me. The next day, just 24 hours after I had been handed the chrome kickstand to the greatest bicycle that had ever raced on blacktop, Dad took it back to the store before I was even out of bed.

I discovered what happened when Scott and I raced outside after wolfing down our Cheerios and opened the garage door to unleash our new stallions, only to discover there was only one bike standing there, resting quietly alone. My brother was always better than me in math and therefore had a head start by calculating the odds favored him as the rightful owner of that lone bicycle. Before I could make a move, he outmaneuvered me by placing a death grip on it, assuring me who the owner was.

Conceding, I ran back inside the house and asked Mom what happened to my bike. "Maybe you should call your dad at work," was her reply. When

I did, he put it to me as most dads are capable of doing—straight and to the point. He said, "You didn't thank me so I took it back." Twice in world history the earth has stopped spinning on its axis. The first time occurred when Joshua held up his staff while the Hebrew armies fought the Amorites. The second time—for me anyway—happened when Dad told me what he'd done.

Dad ended up bringing the bike back home that evening once he realized my repentance on the phone was sincere. I realized many years later, once I became a father, that returning the bike was most likely his plan all along.

I harvested a lot of data from those early childhood mistakes that remained stored in my memory banks; like the day I came into the house and heard Mom warn me not to eat the freshly baked cookies until after dinner. I had every intention of obeying, but they sat there on the countertop, lonely and unguarded and beckoning me after she walked out of the kitchen. I learned a valuable life lesson that day. When you lie to your mom, always remember to remove any incriminating evidence that could be used against you. In my case, I forgot to wipe off the cookie crumbs that affixed themselves to my shirt by some unseen magical tape. After she reappeared, she questioned me, asking if I'd eaten any cookies. I assured her I had not, as any kid would do when his survival instincts kick in, to which she pointed to my shirt. It's a bit vague now, but I think that led to my first experience of having my mouth washed out with soap, which was the punishment for lying.

I didn't cuss back then as a young boy because someone told me that I'd go straight to hell if I ever said the words "shut up" or "stupid." I do remember, though, calling my second youngest brother, Todd, a "dumb butt" at one time, which in those days was considered a double-damnation word—as far as Mom was concerned.

I jokingly tell people that I cuss now because the unofficial missionary handbook states it's OK to swear three times per year. The types of words we're allowed to use and when to self-express is a trade secret. Actually, it tends to happen while we're working on a broken-down vehicle or dodging obstinate jeepney and taxi drivers while navigating through traffic.

My childhood continued somewhat unhampered for a few years until it was unintentionally hijacked when my parents decided to move my three younger brothers and me from northern Idaho to eastern Oregon where my dad received an offer to take over his father's business in the town of Baker because he was planning to retire. I remember driving for hours and hours as I lay in the back of our cream-colored Chevrolet station wagon until we finally pulled into the driveway of an empty house sitting at the end of Park Street in a subdivision called Cedar Acres. It was three times larger than the house we had come from and I was told it would be our new home. Mom and Dad gave me permission to pick out my own bedroom.

In retrospect, I suppose the experiences of living in Oregon weren't all that different from my life in northern Idaho once we got settled. It was just a different town under the same sky. I entered 4th grade when we resettled in Baker, and had no complaints other than the natural awkwardness of trying to make new friends. My brothers and I built forts, played in irrigation ditches that fed the surrounding alfalfa fields, and jumped our bicycles over makeshift wooden ramps. I joined the swim team, collected newspapers for the newspaper drive, shoveled snow, helped friends with their paper routes, played street basketball and baseball with other kids living on our block, and mowed some lawns for pocket money so I could go to the cinema and buy beef jerky. Dad took us fishing during the summer, and we learned how to shoot ground squirrels with our .22 caliber rifles—after we passed the required hunters safety course.

At times, I immersed myself into books that helped expand my childhood world of adventures. My personal favorite was the story about Billy and his two Redbone hounds, Little Ann and Old Dan, chasing coons in the Ozark Mountains of Oklahoma as described by Wilson Rawls in his book *Where the Red Fern Grows*—which I read again and again. In *My Side of the Mountain* Jean Craighead George tells the story about young Sam Gribley who hears the call of the wild and decides to run away from home. He ends up in the Catskill Mountains where he takes up residence in a hollowed-out tree and learns to endure the winter using wilderness survival skills he read about in a book at the public library. I don't recall if I ever planned to run away from home. I suppose the closest I may have considered it came after Mom washed my mouth out with soap. I probably wouldn't have gotten very far, but the story about Sam gave me a glimpse of what it might have been like to tie a bandana around a thin tree branch, fill it with cookies and peanut butter sandwiches, and head down the street.

Church was a mainstay for us, and we went faithfully every Sunday. I'm not sure if I recall any of the sermons I heard, but at the close of every service we were exhorted by the pastor to repent and recommit our lives to Christ down at the altar. One Sunday evening, the Christian apocalyptic movie *A Thief in the Night* was shown and I remember it literally scared the hell out of us kids. An altar call was given when the whirling and clacking Bell & Howell film projector was turned off at the end of the movie. That scene where Patty fell off the dam as her "friends" tried to capture her and make her take the mark of the beast, only to wake up from a dream and find out the rapture had really happened, caused every kid under the age of 16 to come back to Jesus—again! I lost count of how many times I recommitted my life down at the altar during those years.

My grandfather happened to be the mayor. The city park was expansive and a favorite place to have fun. The parades were exciting, people were friendly, and parents didn't need to worry about what side of town their kids were playing in. We were true "free range" kids.

* * *

Aside from the normalcy that typical kids experienced while growing up in any small town during the early 70s, there was nothing particularly special about those years that stood out as unique or spectacular. That is, until my 14th Christmas, when my parents gave me a present that was entirely unexpected.

I received snow skiing lessons at a small resort located about 45 minutes from town. It was tucked in the back corner of the scenic Elkhorn Mountains that rise several thousand feet over Baker Valley, opposite the Wallowa Mountains standing in solemn snow-capped adornment on the adjacent horizon. Scott and Todd were included and the three of us shared the gift, which was a four-lesson package, inclusive of lift tickets and equipment rentals. Most kids have a general idea of what gifts to expect for Christmas, just like Ralphie in the classic movie *A Christmas Story* who got his Red Ryder BB Gun rifle—despite his mom being convinced he'd shoot someone's eye out. Thankfully, dads tend to prevail over things like that as it relates to their sons, and Ralphie's dad pulled through and secretly bought the gun. Ralphie's mom was just as surprised as he was.

I don't know if my parents conspired over the gift they gave us that particular Christmas, or if one of them prevailed over the other's objection like Ralphie's father. We had no idea what to think or how to respond. Getting an erector set, a new board game, or even a 10-speed bicycle would have generated a livelier response of gratitude. Snow skiing? We had never thought about skiing. In fact, we'd hadn't even tried ice skating for that matter.

The only snow adventure we'd experienced was hooky-bobbing behind cars and sliding down the snow-covered sides of the local gravel pit on giant truck tire inner tubes. Weekend entertainment during winter months in eastern Oregon, long before the era of the Internet and smart phones, was either spent indoors playing board games like LIFE, Scrabble, Battleship and endless hours of Monopoly, or my brothers and I were outside building snow forts. Snow skiing was nowhere on our radar screens. We grew up in a small town with an economy that revolved around cattle ranching and logging. Who skied?! I only knew of one red-haired kid in school who said he skied a few times at some place called Anthony Lakes.

I guess my brothers and I tried to play off our parent's enthusiasm in order to show some appreciation. Once the initial shock subsided, my dad said the lessons came with a condition. It wasn't a warning about wearing long underwear under our clothes to stay warm, or hats on our heads for fear we'd come down with bronchitis. It came as a simple provision that seemed to hint at the future when he said, "We're only paying for these four lessons. If you want to continue skiing afterward then it's your responsibility to pay for everything."

* * *

I didn't know what to expect after we paid the $5 fee to ride a school bus up to the resort and made our way to the rental shop where some guy in a multicolored ski hat helped us get into ski boots that fit correctly. He then handed each of us as set of skis and poles, which we dragged behind us to the designated ski school area where we joined a group of other people. I recall the instructor being incredibly patient. She tried to ease our anxiety, which was helpful because we believed this woman was going to demonstrate that it was actually possible to remain standing upright without falling over once we were attached to the skis. For a beginner, this is actually a very big thing. For the most part we spent the first lesson on the ground with our arms and legs splayed out in various designs of static chaos, caused by what we'd considered at that time to be an intense wipeout, but in truth we'd merely fallen over while attempting high speed maneuvers that were clocked at 2 mph.

The one thing that frustrated me throughout the lessons were my fellow ski school classmates. It didn't take long to realize the success of our ability to learn how to ski was directly proportional to the skill level of the most uncoordinated person in our group. We'd spend fifteen minutes helping some guy stand up after he'd fallen over and getting him back into his Spademan bindings, only to ski another 20 feet and do it all over again when he lost his balance for the umpteenth time. I think it took us two weeks to get down the first run. I was itching to break free of the pack, not necessarily because I had the skills, but because I felt like I was being held back by some guy who just couldn't figure it out, while the rest of us had to manage his descent down the run.

I give a lot of credit to the instructor who did a great job encouraging us as we desperately tried to figure out how to make our bodies sync with the equipment so we could navigate down a beginner run, despite being fledgling novices. However, introductory lessons only cover the very basics. I learned to ski, really ski that is, by watching other people and my goal was to learn how to ski moguls.

Only a handful of people on any given day at a ski resort possess the skill and balance to navigate a mogul field down a black diamond run. Many people can ski those runs, but only a few have the coordination and agility to navigate it with fluid perfection. I wanted to be like those people and eventually, after a lot of practice over the next couple of years while spending almost every weekend on the slopes, my brothers and I achieved that skill level.

The only way to acquire that skill, however, is by falling a lot. I remember a comment made by a friend after a day of skiing claiming he hadn't fallen once, attempting to validate how good he was. We quietly laughed and explained that he had it all wrong. The only way he could learn to become a good skier was to take risks and go beyond his comfort level, which would require a few wipeouts. There's a psychological thing that happens while skiing. The tendency is to lean backwards, especially if you're on the precipice of a black diamond run. Your mind is thinking *Whoa, hold on there and lean back because you're headed downhill.* A good skier will lean forward and drive the skis down through the moguls.

The ultimate mogul run at Anthony Lakes was *Rock Garden*. The sign at the top said, "Warning, you will die!" because it was merciless and no one had any business attempting to ski its face unless they knew what they were getting into. It was incredibly intimidating, being situated directly under the chairlift where people watched it eat novices for lunch as the moguls reached up and tackled them without mercy. Your heart beats so strong while standing at the top of the run that your goggles vibrate. During rare moments when an expert took that run and made it seem effortless, you could almost audibly hear those watching from the lift whisper to themselves that they'd give anything to ski like that.

Many books and articles have been written about professional sports and the spiritual analogies we can glean from them. Generally, snow skiing isn't used in those analogies because a larger percentage of the population can better relate to football or basketball. Skiing helped me be a risk taker, and this attitude transferred into my life as a missionary. I learned to lean into opportunities as they came along just as I leaned into the moguls. I also learned that not every opportunity presented on the mission field is necessarily from the Lord, and it takes experience and prayerful discernment to say "No," just as an expert skier will choose to stay off a black diamond run if his knees are sore, or if he feels his rhythm has been a bit out of sync that day. He doesn't need to take the run just because he's a highly-advanced skier. He'll wait for another day—a time when everything synchronizes.

Skiing became my life during my teenage years, and everything else took second place. We worshiped clear weather days when the air was so clear that it made the color of the green pine trees stand out in vibrant contrast against the background sky infused with a deep blue. Typically, my brothers and I were the first ones on the chairlift in the morning when the Ski Patrol formally opened the mountain, and we were usually the last ones off the mountain at the end of the day.

A lot of guys who were my age at that time were into team sports or hunting and fishing. I did those things and enjoyed them, but skiing was my Eden. I'm not sure why. Maybe it touched so many things—the outdoors, adventure, risk, fear, excitement, and an independence that didn't succumb to group pressure. Any avid skier will tell you, there is nothing like standing atop a ski run while cold polished air sparkles around you as if tiny "crystals of ice were floating in it," as Thoreau wrote, while looking down over a new mantle of fresh snow with lodge pole pines and tamaracks standing at attention on either side—waiting to guide you down a run.

I eagerly looked forward to getting up on the mountain every weekend, but being able to do so depended on one very important thing—earning enough money to fund my new passion because skiing is expensive. And that's when I was immersed into a whole new series of adventures.

2

Stupid is as Stupid Does

The following summer I was fortunate enough to land a job at the local truck stop which was situated at the base of the main exit into town right off the interstate freeway. While it was nothing glamorous, I got paid every two weeks and the money earned was set aside to buy my first set of ski equipment. It was a busy place with a great deal of activity due to countless travelers and long haul truckers who stopped for fuel, food, and restroom breaks. Two other gas stations sat adjacent to each other across the street, and I ended up working at all three places during the next couple of years— full time during the summer months and part time the rest of the year.

I was 15 years old when I began working at the truck stop and was assigned the graveyard shift, which was actually illegal, but I didn't know that at the time and the owner didn't realize I was an underage minor because he never asked for a work permit, which I could get when I turned 16. I'd been hired as a pearl diver, which was slang for a person who washes dishes, and it became entirely evident on my first day that there's no job lower in a truck stop. The short order cooks comped me a meal every shift, which meant I could choose anything on the menu, and I was given the freedom to drink as many Cokes as I wanted or blend myself a thick chocolate milkshake during slow times.

Thankfully, I was able to transfer out of the kitchen after a couple of months and started pumping gas at the station attached to the back of the restaurant. A few weeks later, two of the waitresses asked if they could talk with me during a break and invited me to meet them at a corner booth in the restaurant lounge area that provided some privacy. They got right to the point and told me that I could earn some extra money if I was willing to be their pimp. I didn't realize they were offering certain services to the truckers who pulled in off the interstate at night for a few hours of sleep in their attached sleeper cabs. A typical integrated semi-truck sleeper cab has a twin bed, microwave oven, and a small refrigerator. Some of the larger cab units even have a small bathroom with a shower. It's basically a tiny private hotel room. I politely said "No" because I didn't know what a pimp was. They laughed, then explained it to me. I bowed out of the idea which was OK with them.

Working in a truck stop was an interesting experience as a teenager and I found myself exposed to some things I hadn't seen before. Aside from the job offer to be a pimp, a co-worker oftentimes set up a water pipe in the small storage room behind the main office where he smoked marijuana while I pumped gas for customers. I never reported him, but I kept hoping the owner would stop in unannounced and discover what he was doing. The local town drunks would come to the restaurant after the bars closed at 2:00 am. Occasionally, when someone got a bit unruly one of the waitresses would walk back to the station and ask me for a steel tipped wooden tire "thumper" which is a billy club truckers used to bang on their tires to check for proper inflation. Then she'd return to the restaurant, stand up on a chair and threaten the drunk to either get out or deal with the club. It worked every time. I'm glad I decided not to be their pimp!

I actually enjoyed pumping fuel and helping the truckers as best I could. I found them to be genuinely friendly people who just wanted someone to talk to after being alone on the road for extended hours. Almost every morning, just before sunrise I walked out to the parking lot where dozens of semis were lined up and knocked on the side of the sleeper cabs of those who requested a wake-up call. Occasionally, one of the truckers would open the back door of his trailer and hand me a bag of potatoes, corn or something they were hauling, which I took home to Mom.

*   *   *

The following summer I transferred to one of the stations across the street where I also pumped gas. It was a much smaller place and quite boring compared to the constant activity of the big truck stop. During those long hours while working alone during the graveyard shift I did what many bored teenage boys did. I started meddling with stuff. There was a vending machine sitting in the small lobby and I figured out how to rock it back and forth with enough momentum to knock a package of M&M's or cookies out of the dispensing slot. Then after transferring to the day shift I figured out how to cheat customers. I noticed that most people don't pay attention to details, and I used this to my advantage.

This was back in the day when gas pumps registered scrolling numbers on mechanical dials—long before today's pumps that display a single digital price, regardless of which nozzle was chosen. Oregon is one of two states that doesn't allow self-service. I guess the state legislature assumed people were either not smart enough to pump their own gas, or thought it would provide jobs to hundreds if not a few thousand people like me who needed work. I had pumped enough gas to estimate how many gallons a typical mid-size to large car would need if the customer wanted a full tank, which was a majority of the purchases. Each gas pump had two nozzles located at opposite sides of the pump with a corresponding price dial. After filling up a car and replacing the nozzle, if I noticed the customer was distracted or not paying attention I asked for the total amount registered on the dials from the other nozzle. For example, if the actual amount pumped was $14.34 I would ask for the $17.67 shown on the other dial and then pocket the difference from the cash register after they drove off. No one ever picked up on what I did so it was virtually foolproof because the number of pumped gallons computed at the end of the day always reconciled with the money in the cash register. I made it all balance when I took out the extra money.

This was a time when gas station attendants would wash windshields, check air pressure in the tires and the oil level. I figured out one day that if I didn't push the dipstick all the way down into the tube it would indicate low oil. My ploy only worked when the customer went around the back of the building to use the restroom. He'd tell me to add a quart of oil then once he was out of sight I'd pick up an empty oil can out of the garbage and pop it into the fill hole. He'd walk out, see the oil can upside down in the fill hole and assumed I'd just dumped in a quart of oil. I then reinserted the dipstick, pushing it all the way in to get a full reading and show it to the customer. He was happy and I pocketed $1.25. The first time I told these stories to my children they looked at me in shock, trying to understand how their dad could have done such a thing. I'm still trying to reconcile my reputation in their eyes.

*   *   *

"Stupid is as stupid does" is the quote made famous by Tom Hanks in the movie *Forrest Gump*. It means that a person isn't stupid per se' but they can be stupid by their actions. Well, that was me at that time in my nonsensical season of teenage life when doing stupid things like cheating people can be like an addictive drug, causing a person to want more and more. After becoming proficient with the dipstick sleight-of-hand trick I decided to move into uncharted territory and started manipulating credit card receipts. I did it by modifying the purchase price imprinted on the carbon copy of the original receipt. This was before the age of electronic transactions when credit cards were processed using a manual imprinter, which made it somewhat easy to modify a number—such as making a one appear to look like a two.

Granted, my plan had an obvious weakness—the customer always drove away with the original top copy receipt, which I hadn't manipulated. I knew the bank would charge him for the modified amount recorded on the carbon copy, which my boss would submit to the credit card company for payment, but I gambled that the customer would never compare his original receipt with the amount listed on his monthly statement. Unfortunately, it was only a matter of time until someone did. One guy checked his statement against his original gas receipts and found an anomaly. He mailed the evidence back to the owner of the gas station, which prompted him to look into the situation further—maybe more out of curiosity than anything else. Once he knew what to look for, he discovered multiple manipulations I'd been doing over the course of an entire summer. I don't know how long he thought about how to handle that problem but I'll give him credit for his masterful decision when he chose to make a very calculated move. Rather than confronting me directly he gathered all the receipts, drove down to our family-owned business, walked in the front door and laid all the evidence on the counter in front of my dad. I was a minor and he had every right to involve my dad based on what I'd done.

I swallowed pretty hard, wondering what was about to unfold when Dad called me into his bedroom after he got home from work that day. Teenagers are experts at coming up with something to minimize what they know is about to come down on them pretty hard, but I was speechless when he showed me the evidence. I had nothing to say. My self-preservation gauge read empty.

Dad did something he usually didn't do, especially considering the gravity of my guilt. He said he would deal with me the following day, which only added more anguish and misery. The next day he picked me up after school and drove us to the gas station. The owner saw Dad park the car and walked out to meet us. The two of them greeted each other and shook hands. I didn't shake any hands. They then engaged in some small talk that adults do while I pretended not to be there. After their short conversation about the weather, the price of gas, the latest international crisis, or whatever things adults talk about in situations like that, my dad paused for a brief moment and then looked directly at me. Then he looked at the other gentlemen and in a bold but humble manner Dad asked the man how much money I'd stolen.

My former boss replied that he honestly didn't know, and then my dad turned to me. "How much money did you steal?" Those two words, "you" and "steal", felt like a pair of grenades going off in my chest. I was laid bare and completely exposed before my own dad and the man I'd worked for as those two words fell like an indictment at my feet. I said that I didn't really know, but confessed it was probably about $100 which back then was a sizable amount of money. Dad didn't say anything as I watched him reach into his back pocket and pull out his wallet. I saw several bills as I glanced into his wallet, but in particular I noticed three or four new hundred dollar bills that looked crisp, as if they'd never been circulated and were fresh from the bank. I realized later that Dad had come prepared.

There are two ways parents can deal with children who make mistakes or do stupid things; enact punitive measures or look for redemptive options. Like most fathers from Dad's generation, he didn't lack in the punitive actions, which my brothers and I deserved during times of stupidity. But in this particular situation Dad chose the latter. He clearly had the lead role and took his position at center stage while I was left in the dark because I hadn't been given a copy of the script. I was not ready for what came next. Dad pulled out a hundred-dollar bill and handed it to the man, then asked if everything was OK. My former boss nodded, and replied with a "Yes." They shook hands, said a few more words that I didn't really hear, then we got in our car and drove home. He never punished me and he wasn't angry. Aside from paying him back the $100 I don't recall that he ever brought it up again.

My story about stealing from that man to fund my skiing adventures didn't end there. Like a stone pulled back in the pocket of a slingshot and let go, that story passes through time, like a rock flying through air, and lands seventeen years in the future where the last sentence of that narrative was written. It happened when God blew the dust off the script and put me back into the story, but as the lead actor, which unfolded during a furlough from the mission field. First, though, I need to work my way through a timeline and share a few more stories that influenced who I am, which helped me emerge from a Christian life that lacked any adventure.

3.

Searching for a Story

I spent my first year out of high school lacking any direction in life, aside from skiing and working, until I found myself a willing participant regarding an unexpected opportunity. The mother of one of my friends casually suggested I apply to the same Christian college he was attending in Oklahoma. I did, and I was accepted, which came as a shock because I wasn't expecting it. A couple of months later I headed east out of Oregon and spent three days driving my '74 Mustang across four states. After arriving at the school, I soon realized that I was a fish out of water coming from a small rural town to a much larger city in the south.

My immersion into college life where incoming freshmen were required to live on campus was almost as much of a culture shock as going to the mission field. So much was different from back home when I compared the campus and the sprawling city to the small-town life I was familiar with. Back home, I fit in and knew almost everyone in town. Here, I didn't know anyone and it didn't take long until I noticed that I looked different than everyone else. In particular, my clothes were a style that no other human being was wearing.

About two weeks after getting settled, one of the resident graduate students living in my dorm invited me to the mall. His name was Dean and he determined I needed some intervention. He led me to the men's clothing section in one of the department stores and stopped next to a display of folded shirts arranged on a table, then pulled a $100 bill out of his wallet and handed it to me. He told me that the bland colored polyester shirts with matching clip-on ties, which lacked any fashion sense, and the swede shoes with the thick translucent polyurethane soles had to go. He explained what a button-down oxford was, why 100% cotton was preferred due to the southern humidity, and why slip-on penny loafers were the best all-around shoe to have. He told me that shirt colors needed to contrast with the pants, and the unpardonable fashion sin at the time was dressing in a similar pant and shirt color that blended together, which is exactly what I'd been wearing.

The school had a dress code policy that required women to wear dresses and men to wear ties. I hadn't realized it, but every time I got dressed for my classes I looked like a dreary overcast morning. A hundred dollars back then was enough to buy three shirts, a couple of real ties and some casual penny loafers. After we got back to the dorm, Dean showed me how to tie a single and double Windsor knot in my necktie, but suggested I stick with the double because more guys went with the triangle shape the double provided. I was trying to keep up with all the new information and just said "OK."

* * *

The college was nationally known because the founder was a famous TV preacher based in Tulsa. I used to watch him when I was a kid on Sunday mornings before we'd go to church. I liked his show because the back-up girl singers were pretty. I likened him to Moses when I first saw him in person during a chapel service. He and the administration seemed like sincere and godly people, and I had the privilege of listening to some incredible speakers during the bi-weekly chapel services. Like a sponge, I soaked up many truths about the Bible that helped shape the foundations of my Christian life beyond what I'd learned in church growing up. Missionaries were occasionally invited as guest speakers, and they wowed the student body as they testified what they'd experienced on mission fields far flung around the world where the gospel hadn't been preached. I also attended services at a growing megachurch with a couple of thousand members who met in the large indoor arena located on the college campus. I lost track of all of the nationally recognized preachers and ministry leaders I heard as they rotated through on their speaking tours.

I was at a nominal place of vulnerability during this time because my heart was being nurtured at a place beyond the Sunday school stories I grew up listening to in church. There were about 100 students in the student body, which at that time numbered about 2,000, who seemed genuinely hungry for God, and I counted myself among them. A Friday evening Vespers service was the highlight of my week when most of those 100 students met in a small campus chapel with a united intent to grow closer to God through worship and listening to inspirational exhortations—all of which was centered around sharing in the Lord's supper. Bob Stamps composed the song "God and Man at Table are Sat Down," which we sang during each service and became a focal point of communion. We were collectively mentored by a godly chaplain on how to cultivate a deeper relationship with Christ. Rarely did God not show up during those Friday evenings in that small campus chapel, because we witnessed that God is drawn to those who choose to make themselves vulnerable.

Many of us were also being deeply influenced by the writings of C.S. Lewis and A.W. Tozer who wrote, "For it is not mere words that nourish the soul, but God Himself, and unless and until the hearers find God in personal experience they are not the better for having heard the truth." In looking back on those days, I believe the hunger experienced by many young bible school students such as myself was more of a response to God's initiating rather than my own, which Tozer summed up by writing, "Before a man can seek God, God must first have sought the man."

* * *

The writings of Tozer and other Christian authors had a profound effect on me, but I found myself growing a bit disillusioned with what for me was becoming a Christian life that seemed rather normal. Strangely, those disillusions were actually being sustained by the stories I was hearing from all of those well-known guest speakers we were listening to. I'll use a skiing analogy to explain.

My brothers and I skied so much growing up that it became boring. I shied away from using the term "expert" to label our skill level, but we were well advanced and could confidently handle any black diamond run whether it was powder or deep moguls. We were up on the mountain almost every weekend while the average skier may only hit the slopes four or five times each year. We skied so much the thrill began to wear off a bit toward the end of each season, so we looked for ways to intensify an experience that had lost its "edge." We had become so proficient in our skill levels that skiing was no longer an adventure for us. As a result, we looked for crazy ways to get the adrenaline rush back—like doing flips off makeshift snow jumps or skiing beyond the boundary zones marked off with warning signs by the mountain management. We may have also inadvertently invented the precursor to the snowboard when we mounted bindings on an elevated wood platform attached to a single ski and used it as a mono ski. It worked great, but we soon tired of that as well.

For some reason, which I didn't understand at the time, I found myself at a place in my Christian walk where I became bored with church, just like I was bored with skiing. I didn't need a spiritual black diamond run to pump up my Christian adrenaline. I just needed my own adventure instead of listening to the adventures of others. Attending church and chapel was like watching a travel show on TV where I heard other people, such as those missionary guest speakers talk about going to exotic places that held intrigue, history, beauty, new friends, new customs, and new tastes—all those things a new adventure has to offer. It's like I was vicariously living a Christian life by listening to other people who actually lived a Christian life beyond attending Sunday school or mailing a check to a ministry that helped street kids in the slums of Rio. In truth, it felt like those stories were a substitute for an authentic story I wanted to call my own.

The story about a friend's experience summed it up best. He signed up for a two-week short term trip with some mission organization, and after returning he invited me to Mazzio's Pizza Parlor for lunch where he shared how he smuggled bibles into China. The narrative was simple enough, but the way he went into expressive detail, explaining how he hid the small bibles inside his backpack and behind the lining of his coat as he entered from Hong Kong into mainland China beckoned me. The story was full of adventure and excitement, fear and faith, and angels battling the forces of darkness as they guarded the team bringing their holy stash into an evil empire that desperately needed God's word. He talked for an hour while my mind created images that served as a backdrop for a story that had been real to him, but secondhand for me. It was almost like listening to someone narrate a James Bond movie. Then after our visit we left the restaurant and everything returned to normal the next day, as if I hadn't even heard the story because I knew I would never experience so grand an adventure as that. Mine was just a general Christian life—not much different than what most other Christians were living.

* * *

It's been said that our 20s are the most difficult times of our lives. Aside from the small percentage of the human population who are goal oriented and discover their purpose in life at the age of five and pursue it like a well-oiled machine, most of us can describe our twenties as "clunky" at best. We make dumb mistakes with a resulting fruit that tends to linger for the rest of our lives. We struggle with debt because we don't understand money, even when well-intended parents or relatives try to advise us. We're wracked with self-doubt and anxiety, and in truth we pretend to be mature but lack the life experience that qualifies us to have wisdom. We try to immerse ourselves into a career but can't seem to figure out how to set boundaries, or we become victims of narcissistic bosses. Some of our friends turn out to be subtly manipulative and we end up serving their egos at our expense. If we're newly married, we try to figure how to live with a spouse when no one taught us how to be married because a comprehensive reference manual titled "How to be Married" has never been written. Actually, I did find a book titled *"How to be Married"* with the subtitle *"Why doesn't marriage come with a manual?"*

That's where I was while trying to sort out things regarding the slippery slope I was descending into my so-called nominal Christian life. One day while sitting in church listening to yet another three-point sermon with pews full of fellow church members, I came to a place where I decided to pull over, get out of the car, toss the keys on the seat and say "I'm done." I wasn't giving up on Christianity, but I decided that unless the construct I'd become a part of could make more sense, which allowed me to be immersed into a narrative involving action rather than just believing something, then I needed a timeout. I likened that season in my life to what John Wimber asked after he got saved, "When do we get to do the stuff?" When asked what "stuff" he was talking about, he replied, "You know. The stuff Jesus did; heal the sick, raise the dead." The pastor responded, "We don't do that stuff anymore." To which Wimber replied, "What do we do then?"

Attending church is safe in many regards. If we're not careful it can put us on a path of minimal resistance and shallow significance because mere attendance tends to provide added value to our Christianity and becomes not the means to an end, but the end itself. For me, there was a clear deficit between what I knew in my heart and what I was doing with this knowledge. No one was able to help me reconcile what I was unable to articulate and the disconnect I was feeling. This was rapidly becoming a growing source not of frustration, but rather a struggle to bridge the gap or validate it. I think I would have come undone if someone had quoted John 15:16 to me; "I have empowered you to bear fruit," which for me was very similar to Nike's "Just Do It" ad campaign. I'd have replied with "Just do what?!" What can I do to make the connection because I wanted to be involved in something that was going to count, and I didn't care if it was small by comparison to what other people we considered modern day Christian heroes were doing. I was looking for a faith experience that went beyond the pews.

Larry Burkette said, "Tithing is an outward expression of an internal witness." I had an internal witness of being a Christian but lacked the understanding to express it outwardly, so one day I decided to do something. My first foray searching for an adventure I could call my own and help connect my faith with something tangible was a flop—or at least it felt that way. Very early one morning, long before most college students were awake, I got into my car and drove to a park along the riverside. I saw a man picking up empty soda cans and place them inside a large transparent plastic garbage bag. It was obvious he was collecting them for their redemption value. He looked a bit scraggly and I assumed he was either homeless or just trying to find something to help make ends meet.

I walked up and offered to buy his cans to which he replied it wasn't necessary. I quickly calculated the value at 5 cents each and figured he had about $3 worth of tin. I offered him triple. He looked at me in shock and said "OK." I handed him $10 and told him that Jesus loved him. My entire interaction with him was no more than one minute and I clearly remember walking away feeling more empty inside than before I approached him. What had I accomplished? Nothing. I felt that it was a complete fumble. I was desperate to somehow demonstrate a work in line with what I was experiencing in my heart. What prompted me was my desire to be authentic and look for an avenue not necessarily to validate my faith, but to express it.

* * *

The plumb line by which I measure experiences I choose to pursue is my tendency to default to wanting to tell God a story someday. I remember telling my parents all the things we'd done when they left my brothers and me with our grandparents for a week in Portland. We helped Grandpa chop wood, rode his tractor, went to the zoo, picked peaches, taught my youngest brother, Eric, how to drown in the bathtub, and other things boys do. They laughed as we relived the week for them and seemed relieved that we all returned home in one piece and hadn't destroyed Grandma's home.

God already knows everything, so I wonder what it will be like to explain our lives to God and tell Him our stories. The summation of our Christian experience can't be based on what others are writing about or the stories they tell. That would be like watching a travel show on TV and seeing images of amazing and beautiful places, yet never getting on a plane and going somewhere, anywhere, to experience it for ourselves. One of my favorite movie scenes is from the Academy Award winning movie *Good Will Hunting* where Sean Maguire, played by Robin Williams, is sitting on a bench with Will and says;

"So, if I asked you about art, you'd probably give me the skinny on every art book ever written. Michelangelo, you know a lot about him. Life's work, political aspirations, and the pope, sexual orientations, the whole works, right? But I'll bet you can't tell me what it smells like in the Sistine Chapel. You've never actually stood there and looked up at that beautiful ceiling;

28

seen that. If I ask you about women, you'd probably give me a syllabus about your personal favorites. But you can't tell me what it feels like to wake up next to a woman and feel truly happy. You're a tough kid. And if I'd ask you about war, you'd probably throw Shakespeare at me, right, 'once more unto the breach dear friends.' But you've never been near one. You've never held your best friend's head in your lap, watch him gasp his last breath looking to you for help. I'd ask you about love, you'd probably quote me a sonnet. But you've never looked at a woman and been totally vulnerable. Known someone that could level you with her eyes, feeling like God put an angel on earth just for you."

Many years ago, I got past feeling that when God calls us to the front of the class it will be to punish us or express disappointment. Rather, I tend to I think He may ask us why we didn't do more with what He entrusted to us. That bothered me, but in a good way. I don't want to stand before God someday and realize I could have done more with my life. By "more" I don't mean quantity, but rather doing something significant. It doesn't need to be noteworthy or momentous. I just want it to be meaningful — to count for something.

A friend of mine told me the first time he ever heard his dad say that he was proud of him was when he was 35-years old. He said he was happy to hear it, but he also shrugged it off saying it was a bit late. It lacked meaning. It didn't seem to count as much as it could have if his dad had told him that while growing up.

I want God to say He's proud of me when He asks me to account for what I did. And when I tell him my stories, like handing a guy $10 for a bag of empty soda cans, I have a sense He's going to remove the idea that we need to feel like we have to meet some great expectation to prevent Him from being disappointed. I'm not so sure God is asking us to account as to why we didn't accomplish something amazing. I think He will make us feel how proud He is of us just for trying, and whether it turned out to be something spectacular, like Billy Graham preaching to millions of people, or a pastor faithfully serving a small flock of people, or a missionary who works tirelessly amongst a people group that never responds to the gospel message, God will personally say "well done."

In his book *To Be Told*, author Dan Allender encourages readers to examine their lives in a search for the story that God is telling through their existence. Allender writes, "We often don't know our own stories because we doubt their existence, dismiss their importance, or we're distracted."

Before my larger story could begin to form and take shape as an adventure, I wanted to share my front row seat with someone special who, at the end of my life, knew what it meant to struggle at times, and to also share in the goodness we created together. It took a trip to the other side of the world to get me on the right path to find my future wife, which actually led me to the end of a water buffalo trail.

4.

Cookie Quandary

I spent six years in Oklahoma before relocating back to my home state of Oregon where I landed a construction job near the growing city of Bend and immersed myself into a new church that was meeting in a high school cafeteria. After attending for about six months an opportunity to participate in a short-term mission trip to the Philippines presented itself. Many people returning from a mission trip reported how impacting their experience was, but how they felt at its peak tends to fade as they move on with their lives. It played out a bit different for me—something that is shared only by people who have gone on to serve as career missionaries. That trip ultimately set me on an adventure that would transcend and define the rest of my life.

I was scheduled to join up with a married couple from the church, who had gone ahead two weeks earlier. They were in Manila, serving at a Filipino church pastored by an American missionary. Unfortunately, they had to cut their trip short and we only had a couple of days together before they flew back to the States. My return ticket was scheduled 30 days later so I ended up spending the entire time on my own without any team members. The host missionary was a bit odd and seemed too preoccupied to deal with me, as if I was a nuisance. So, he arranged for me to visit churches affiliated with his organization in the outlying provinces (*bundok—a Tagalog word borrowed by American GIs stationed in the Philippines during WWII who spelled it "boondock" and introduced it as an American slang term meaning "out in the sticks."*)

Two days later I was ushered onto an overnight bus headed north out of Manila. No one accompanied me and I sat on the bus without any idea of where I was headed or why. Furthermore, I wasn't given an introduction or even a brief orientation regarding the cultural experience into which I was being thrust into. I was simply told not to get off until the bus arrived at its final destination. I tried to stay warm while the air-conditioner blasted at its maximum subzero setting and did my best to avoid watching the slaughter-fest horror movies playing at full volume on a TV suspended above the driver's head. I finally tumbled out of the bus with frozen appendages ten hours later into the relief of the warm tropical weather.

Memories of the several days I spent in that place are a blur because I didn't have enough sense to decline the glass of lukewarm water served at dinner despite noticing it had a subtle brown color to it. I prayed for God to take my life the following morning and spent the remainder of that week in a bed, which had been strategically placed near a bathroom. My hosts finally got me to a doctor who determined I had come down with amoebic dysentery and prescribed metronidazole which enabled me to get back to Manila.

Once I arrived in Manila I was given two days to recover before someone put me on another bus headed to the province of Bulacan where I was greeted by an overly enthusiastic group of people who received me as an American evangelist. I was way out of my comfort zone and didn't understand the reason for the label they'd attached to me. I wasn't an evangelist by any stretch of the imagination. Maybe theirs, but certainly not mine. I did my best to downplay the title, which was greatly helped when not a single person came to the outdoor "crusade" scheduled the next day after they toured me around the city in a Jeepney—while someone with a loud speaker wired to the engine battery kept yelling into a microphone, inviting people to come and hear the American evangelist preach.

I stayed with a hospitable Filipino family, and I really enjoyed the week I spent with them and meeting other church members, including their pastor who was young and quite friendly. I was feeling much better after the dysentery episode, but I determined that any liquid intake would be limited to an assortment of bottled soft drinks because I knew it was safer than water. We had several bible studies together and I showed a couple of old Billy Graham crusade movies inside their church. Those movies were the only thing with which I'd been equipped by the church in Manila when they handed me a portable film projector and a stack of round tin cans containing reels of film. I was exhorted to show the movies and make an altar call, and I was surprised that people actually responded. I guess I was an evangelist after all.

Two days before I was scheduled to return to Manila, I shared a simple exhortation at an informal bible study for a few people who gathered in the church. Afterward, I decided to take a walk along a well-worn dirt path behind the church that was used by men leading their water buffalo (*carabaos*) out to plow the rice fields early in the mornings. I enjoyed taking walks by myself, which I started doing in college, because it was a time for me to talk to God and practice listening for a response. My prayer that evening was an admission to the Lord that I wanted to return to the Philippines and serve as a full-time missionary, which I followed with a request. I didn't want to return alone, so I asked the Lord to find me a wife.

Each of us have probably experienced two or three times in our lives when we were fairly confident that we'd clearly heard God's voice. As I made my way down that carabao path, I sensed an inner voice resonating within me that felt more like an impression. The voice said, "You will find your future wife at the singles group of the church your brother is attending in Portland." That definitely got my attention and I sincerely believed it was the Lord, so I hung on to it, trusting its significance.

* * *

My life in the States at that time was still transitory and I lacked direction regarding a career or even where to settle. So, it wasn't too difficult to leave the construction job in central Oregon after returning from the Philippines. I packed my car and showed up at my brother's apartment in Portland, asking to stay in his spare bedroom.

He took me in—although he couldn't really turn me away since I was his brother—and I began searching for a job, primarily by scouring through the help wanted ads in the Oregonian. Nothing worthwhile materialized until I drove down to the employment office and noticed a job opening for "factory production assistants." The name of the company wasn't listed, but the employment office had been contracted for the screening and interviews. I approached a guy sitting behind a desk off to one side and inquired about the posting. He told me the position was with Nabisco, which had a factory on the northeast side of the city, and explained the job involved packing cookies. He asked if I had any experience in production line assembly work. I replied that I had.

* * *

Although it may appear I'm taking my narrative down a rabbit trail, I decided to include the following brief story about the time I spent working for a deceptive Christian huckster. Strangely enough, it ties in with some inspiration I received while packing cookies for Nabisco.

One of the temporary jobs I'd held while living in Oklahoma was working at a mail processing center under contract to print and mail ministry letters for a TV evangelist based in Texas. We sorted as many as 30,000 letters a day, which were sent to donors in all 50 states. It was a relatively boring job, with the exception of a strange contraption sitting in the center of the large room where we worked that provided us with some entertainment. It was an antiquated green-colored envelope stuffing machine, which could have been used as a set piece for a science fiction "B" movie. It was about the size of a pickup truck and it's hard to explain exactly how it worked with all the armatures and suction cups and the noise that thing made once it was turned on. If everything went smoothly, which rarely happened, it was quite the sight to watch as it took on a life of its own—stuffing thousands of pre-folded letters into envelopes during an eight-hour shift.

I was in charge of the presort department and my job description required me to sort thousands of sealed envelopes by zip code in order to prep them for bulk mailing using classification stickers, rubber bands and plastic mail trays provided by the U.S. Post Office.

We'd shake our heads at times reading some of the letters that TV preacher sent out. The ministry appeared to be legitimate on the surface, and perhaps some of it was, but that TV evangelist sure knew how to milk the cash cow. Most of it was based on gimmicks designed to manipulate people into sending money. One letter in particular claimed he'd prayed over some pieces of cloth—referencing the story of people bringing Paul handkerchiefs in Acts 19, asking God to anoint them. The recipient was to place that cloth, which had been mailed to them, on anything they felt needed to be anointed so he or she could receive a blessing. Another letter contained clear oil sealed in a small transparent plastic sachet. If I remember correctly, people were instructed to anoint their wallet with the oil and pray for a financial blessing, which would hopefully result in sending more money to the preacher man. The evangelist was based in Dallas and we were in Tulsa. Our supervisor told us the oil packets and bundled cloths—mailed to donors from our center—had been sourced locally and the preacher man hadn't been within a hundred miles of them. Every week we'd read his newest letter, many of which contained some manipulative gimmick or incentive for people to send in more money. At one point, it was estimated his ministry brought in close to $80 million annually. I never liked the guy when I watched him on TV, and he seemed like a charlatan.

In a room, adjacent from where I worked, were a dozen women who sat at tables removing checks from preprinted return envelopes, which donors had mailed back to this evangelist. Someone determined that people were more apt to make a donation if a preprinted return envelope was included with the letters mailed to his supporters. Actually, the return address was our center in Tulsa where donations were also processed. Nothing went to Dallas.

The ministry grew to such an extent that our facility couldn't effectively process the tens of thousands of envelopes arriving each month full of donations. Someone eventually came up with an idea to have all return envelopes printed with the bank's address located in downtown Tulsa where bank employees would extract the checks for immediate deposit. The bank, obviously, had no interest in reading the letters and only dealt with the money. So, I'd drive to the bank each afternoon to pick up duffel bags packed with the opened letters and deliver them to the women sitting at those tables at our facility who reviewed them and decided if any needed a reply. It was difficult as a Christian listening to bank employees laugh and mock Christianity as they saw the gullibility of people responding to manipulative gimmicks created to solicit tens of millions of dollars. A couple of years after I left that company I learned the preacher guy was later exposed as a fraud by a TV investigative news show and his entire ministry imploded.

* * *

It was the introduction of Chunky Chocolate Chips Ahoy cookies to the snack-food marketplace that helped me get the job at Nabisco. Apparently, the few months I'd spent stuffing prayer cloths and oil sachets convinced the interviewer I was an experienced production line worker and qualified to pack cookies. The job was temporary and I was told that any chance of it extending long term was based entirely on the success of that new cookie.

On the first day I reported to work, I expected to see a lot of automation and was surprised to find equipment I guessed to be several decades old. The factory appeared to have been built sometime in the 1940s. Although everything looked clean, it was definitely not an automated process and I realized why people were being hired. Workers were positioned alongside six-foot-wide rubberized conveyor belts that were slowly emerging from two fifty-foot-long ovens carrying cookies—thousands of cookies. Workers grabbed cookies by the handful as they came down the line and placed them on a white folded cardboard liner. Then they would slide the whole thing inside individually printed cookie bags, which were tossed onto a separate belt, and sent down to the shipping area.

Thankfully the shift supervisors allowed those of us who were new hires to work on each packing line in the factory; such as the regular Chips Ahoy cookie line and the Saltine cracker line. The Wheat Thins and Chicken-in-a-Biskit cracker lines were fully automated, and a few of the old entrenched union guys worked those lines in a separate part of the factory.

The hardest part of the job was packing Oreos, which is considered America's favorite cookie. Although the ingredients are a trade secret we were told the white center is a combination of lard and sugar and, therefore, the pressed cookies pass through a refrigerated cooling tunnel after emerging from the oven, which keeps the white filling from melting and falling apart so it can be packed.

The manual dexterity and coordination necessary to pack Oreos required considerable concentration. As I stepped up to the line for my initial training I was instructed to grab a clear cellophane packaging bag between my thumb and middle finger—two at a time, one in each hand. Then I had to "snap" the bag open using the same motion as when you snap your fingers, which made it pop open, then slip it onto a stainless-steel tray moving down the line adjacent to rows of chilled cookies moving on a conveyor belt. After situating the bag onto the tray, we had to pick up two rows of Oreos and place them on a corrugated plastic liner that held the cookies inside the package. This was all prep work for the next machine that pushed the cookie filled liner into the cellophane package held open by the tray. I think an experienced line operator could successfully negotiate packing a bag of Oreos every 2 seconds. I was clocked at 3 minutes per bag.

Learning how to pop open the bags and get them positioned quickly enough was frustrating, if not somewhat humorous. Perhaps you've seen the famous factory scene from the old *I Love Lucy* TV show where Lucy and Ethel attempt to wrap chocolates in a candy factory while trying to keep up with a conveyor belt putting out more chocolates than they could manage. I identified with Lucy because it only took a few minutes for me and my fellow trainees to cause a fiasco.

When the supervisor first escorted us to the Oreo line for our initial training I noticed another guy following behind us pulling a large 50-gallon yellow plastic garbage can mounted on wheels. And, strangely, he carried a snow shovel in his right hand. I didn't make the connection until the cookie avalanche started a few minutes after we were put on the line for our first Oreo packing session. Once the supervisor showed us how to pack the cookies and stepped back out of the way, it only took a few brief moments until my fellow trainees and I had caused the mother of all cookie jams! As hard as we tried, we simply could not get the cellophane bags opened and mounted on the trays fast enough. Meanwhile the cookies kept coming. I was shocked as I watched the supervisor grab handfuls of Oreos off the line and throw them onto the floor because unpacked cookies couldn't proceed down the line to the sealing machine. I realized what the snow shovel was for when the other guy started shoveling piles of cookies off the floor and dumped them into his big garbage can. Later we asked what happens to all those cookies that end up on the floor. He joked and told us they're ground up and used for "Cookies and Cream ice cream."

* * *

As I stood along those conveyor lines, packing thousands of cookies day after day, the job became incredibly boring—caused by hours of mindless repetition. Once I learned to do the job, I started thinking about the rest of my life. And strangely enough, my thoughts were entirely prompted by the people standing next to me in that factory. I realized I didn't want my life to be normal—at least not in the sense that the people around me were living an apparently normal life. It was fine for them and I wasn't judging them at all because they seemed content, but I was standing next to people who had been doing the same thing for 20 years! They were making good money, had full medical benefits, union-secured retirements, and every Friday several of the long-term workers pulled their RVs into the employee parking lot ready to head off for the weekend after clocking out. I simply couldn't do it. I refused to let that job become the framework for my life. I needed to be intentional about the story I wanted to live and it didn't involve packing cookies for $25 per hour or even $50 per hour working overtime, which was a lot of money at the time. I realized while standing in front of those cookie lines that my greatest adversary was going to be myself if I didn't pursue my own story—something that involved an adventure.

* * *

Each day while working my shifts at Nabisco I remembered the impression I'd received from God regarding my future wife, and things started to unfold much to my delight. A friend introduced me to a girl who lived and worked across the Columbia River over in Vancouver. We started dating and I felt that I was on track with what God had instructed me along that carabao trail.

Now, in honor of my wife, I'll keep this part of the story brief. I dated that girl for about four months and enjoyed the time I spent with her, and her parents whom she lived with. I felt very much welcomed into their family and enjoyed spending time at their beautiful home situated among the pine trees on the outskirts of the city. At some point, I determined she was the one I wanted to marry, and concluded that I was within a relatively close geographical proximity to God's instructions for me to find my wife in Portland. After all, I reasoned, Vancouver is adjacent to Portland—separated only by the river—and is considered a bedroom community. However, I kind of skipped over the part where God told me that I'd find her in the singles group at the church my brother was attending. After dating her a few months I looked at engagement rings and was close to picking one out when I decided it was probably a good idea to honor a previous promise I'd made before taking the plunge.

My brother, Scott, with whom I had initially been sharing the apartment, had relocated to another city and my youngest brother, Eric, had moved in with me. I told Eric that I was thinking about asking my girlfriend to marry me and asked him to meet her. The three of us enjoyed a dinner together a few days later and I confided to him afterward that I'd appreciate his thoughts about my marrying her. This was prompted from my college days when three friends and I made a vow that we'd never marry someone without asking other people close to us what they really thought, because a mutual friend had gotten married even though everyone believed it was a mistake, but no one was willing to say anything. So, I asked my brother and gave him permission to be honest. The dialog unfolded exactly like this;

"Well, I have one word." He said.

I replied with an odd expression and said, "What?"

He repeated himself and said that he had only one word for me.

"OK..." I slowly replied with a hint of caution in my voice. "What's the word?"

There was a long pause, maybe for added dramatic effect, then he said the one word, "Life."

"Huh?" I asked.

Eric looked me in the eye and said, "If you marry that girl it will be for life."

That single word suddenly put everything into perspective. I didn't love that girl enough to be married to her for the rest of my life.

5.

Earth Angel

I decided to put cookies behind me and refocus on what I believed the Lord had instructed me to do. I broke up with my girlfriend after hearing Eric's one-word realignment exhortation, found a new job, and started attending the singles group at my brother's church, which ran about 100 people weekly. I felt confident the high number favored my hopes of finding a wife, and I'll admit that I was proactive in carefully considering every girl who walked in the door. Sadly, I had virtually given up hope after almost a year because I hadn't met any girl that I was even remotely interested in—until a new girl showed up one day after Christmas break. She sure had my attention as she sat in front of me and my heart skipped a beat during the meet and greet time.

Krys was from the very small town of Troy, Montana and was attending Lewis & Clark College situated in Portland's southwest hills. It turns out that she had a similar love for snow skiing. This was an obvious plus, but the stars really started to align when I mentioned that I used to live in northern Idaho, specifically Bonners Ferry. She smiled and said that she attended a church with her family in Bonners Ferry, which was 20 miles from where she grew up next to the Montana-Idaho state line west of Troy.

The circumstances of meeting Krys was intriguing because two weeks before our introduction the singles pastor asked if I'd be willing to help lead an occasional bible study over at Lewis & Clark College. Apparently, the church had received a request for some assistance from the Fellowship of Christian Athletes (FCA) campus lead person at Lewis & Clark who was filling in temporarily until the position was filled. I mentioned to Krys that I might be helping lead a bible study for FCA at her school and briefly shared what the singles pastor and I had discussed. She smiled and confided that she was the one who had contacted the church asking for help.

The intrigue grew even more so when Krys told me where she lived with two roommates—an apartment in the complex adjacent to Eric and me. Not only had God directed me to the church singles group in Portland, He had also placed us in apartments that were literally 75 feet from each other. We had been living almost next door to each other for more than a year.

I had a hard time paying attention to anything else during the rest of the evening. I knew I had met someone special and waited for the right time to ask her out which came a couple weeks later—an invitation to go night skiing at Ski Bowl up on Mt. Hood. We had fun and I was impressed that she could follow me down any black diamond run. Krys has always been quite athletic and in good shape. She played basketball in high school and was a member of the women's track and field team for Lewis & Clark. She ran almost every day, and at the time she was also swimming quite a bit at the college.

The more I got to know Krys the more time I wanted to spend with her. She was very much a small-town girl with a kind and simple approach to life. Krys grew up in a house made from rough-sawn lumber without running water or electricity. Interior lighting was provided by propane gas lights, with an attached mantle to control brightness, which were hung from exposed ceiling joists. Solar panels on the roof charged several car batteries in the sun room situated off the front of the kitchen. The refrigerator ran on propane, using ammonia as a coolant, while a back-up generator powered the house whenever the battery output was unable to meet the electrical demand.

Just prior to my first visit to her home, Krys confided they had used an outhouse for years, only recently converting it to house the generator. The homestead—situated amongst 50' tall cedar and pine trees—is about 500 feet in elevation above the Kootenai River; 7 miles west of where the Yaak River dumps into the Kootenai River, on Old Highway-2 in the southern part of the Purcell Mountains which extend down from Canada. It's a sportsman's paradise with vast beautiful scenery. However, the economy is historically depressed, and the locals referred to the area as "poverty with a view."

Eric had already met Krys since we were attending the same church and he was accustomed to seeing her come over to our apartment to visit me. I also introduced her to my parents when we drove over to visit them in Central Oregon for a weekend. Everything was going well and we dated for 3–4 months until I suddenly and abruptly broke up with her. I'm not sure why exactly, but it was quick and to the point. I wasn't mean or disrespectful, I just decided she wasn't the one, and was determined to be honest with her and end it. I know she was surprised and I don't really remember her getting angry with me other than asking why, for which I didn't really have a good answer.

I walked down to my car the following morning to leave for work and found something under the windshield wiper. It was a zip-lock bag full of freshly baked cookies with a handwritten note stuffed inside. The note said, "Can we still be friends? - Krys."

I really struggled with being overweight when I was a kid. During my junior year in high school I decided to do something about it and lost 75 pounds in 9 months. This resulted in a growing self-confidence and I started asking girls out on dates, which I'd previously been too embarrassed to do. I experienced break ups with girls in the past, some initiated by them and others by me, but I'd never had a girl reach out to me after a break up and ask to be friends. The cookies and note really threw me. That was new and I didn't know what to do. I thought about it as I drove to work that morning, and decided to mention it to Eric later that evening.

"Eric, I broke up with Krys last night."

"Oh."

"Remember when I asked you about my last girlfriend and I wanted to know your honest thoughts about her?"

"Yep." Was his short reply.

"Well, what did you think about Krys?" I asked. "You met her and spent more time with her than the previous girl."

"Honestly?" He asked.

"Yeah, be honest. What can you say about Krys?"

Eric is 7 years younger than me, and as a general rule, older brothers usually don't ask their younger siblings for advice about girls. I was viewing the exchange as more of a conversation piece rather than actually seeking advice, but that took a turn when Eric said something that left me hanging once again.

He said, "She's the one."

Obviously, we can't see our own expressions, but I assumed the one I had on my face was the look of shocked disbelief as I realized he was right and I'd broken up with the woman God wanted me to marry. I looked at Eric and slowly said, "I know."

I think I was on my knees when Krys' roommate opened the door to their apartment after I rang the doorbell. She turned and told Krys there was someone to see her. We've always been sincere and genuine when we apologize to each other and I think Krys saw that I was being honest and contrite. Thankfully, she took me back and forgave me as if I had never broken up with her. (I asked for her narrative of the events after I wrote this section. She replied that she took me back *only* after I admitted I'd been an idiot!)

* * *

Krys graduated from college a few months later and headed to Central America on a summer mission trip with a Christian organization to help build a church. After leaving Nabisco I labored at a new job, which didn't hold out any prospects for a career, but it paid the rent and took care of my needs. During the two months Krys was away, the lyrics of Leo Sayer's classic song summed up what I was feeling; "I miss you ev'ry single day... I love you more than words can say" and I did my best to express that in several letters I mailed to her. It didn't take long until I asked her to marry me soon after she returned. We were married nine months later in June and moved into a small apartment located in a west side bedroom community of Portland.

Krys landed an excellent job working as a Spanish interpreter for the county health department, which served migrant and seasonal farm workers. I gave notice and left my job after interviewing for a county warehouse manager position and beating out 250 other applicants. It was the most boring job I'd ever had and I spent hours with absolutely nothing to do. The job description ran about three sentences and the position was a testimony of an incredibly inefficient and wasteful use of county funds. They had two people working full-time doing what one guy could have done in two hours, part-time every other day. It was pathetic, but the pay and benefits were great. It was also a union job with guaranteed permanent job security for life along with all the typical union benefits and retirement packages. As a new hire, I was placed on an automatic six-month probationary period followed by permanent membership as long as I didn't commit any gross mistakes.

* * *

Everyone has a story to tell, but each of us tend to withhold the depth of our narratives as we walk through various seasons of our lives because we believe our listeners simply can't relate to what we've experienced. This is especially true for Christians as we try to associate God's involvement with those stories, and we fear people may doubt them. To some extent as I look back, I believe the stories I had experienced up to this point—the accumulation of my childhood adventures, experiencing a disconnect at bible college, repositioning myself to obey God's direction to find my spouse—became the basis for finding myself in a story I wasn't anticipating.

The catalyst that led us to the mission field began to unfold through a problem that developed at my workplace, although it took a while for me to recognize how God's hand was involved. I was still in my probation period when a storm began to build, which actually started in church. During a Sunday evening service, I felt convicted about the course we were on as a newly married couple. We were earning good salaries, had a new car and a nicely furnished apartment—all of which propped up a growing complacency that seemed to minimize the desire for an adventure we could call our own. Although we had talked about the mission field before we were married, it has been relegated into the background of our lives and only mentioned during a rare topic of discussion once the honeymoon was over and we'd settled into our jobs. We even considered buying a new house.

The pastor had set a time for prayer towards the end of the service so I held my wife's hand and led us in a prayer, asking God to forgive me. Then,

I said something I wasn't expecting nor had really planned. Tears came to my eyes and I prayed, "Lord, whatever it takes, get us on the mission field."

One of the people who had also interviewed for the position I now held at the county was the only guy who worked with me in the warehouse. He'd been passed over and denied a promotion, which would have included a substantial pay raise. I was a new hire from the outside and, therefore, his newly appointed boss.

About three months into the job I received a call by the senior administrator who was over our department. I'd never met him before and was instructed to report to his downtown office the following morning. I was dumbfounded to hear him lay out several accusations based on the false testimony of my assistant who had been secretly undermining and slandering me. Furthermore, he had conspired with my immediate supervisor who supported the accusations—thus the reason for being called to the meeting.

I had been accused of negligence as it related to competence and job performance, but no evidence of what I had done wrong was provided—only corroborating testimony from my assistant and my supervisor was brought against me. I was given an ultimatum; I had 30 days to demonstrate I was proficient to do the job or I'd be fired.

My supervisor, who had a second-floor office above mine, and my assistant barely spoke to me during those 30-days, and I soon realized their palpable contempt was based on a personal agenda, which I believed stemmed from the fact I was a Christian. I knew there was nothing I could do to further validate my competency to the senior administrator, and I struggled to figure out how to demonstrate I was in fact doing a good job, regardless of what I'd been accused of.

* * *

The situation was troubling and I remember finding some encouragement from a quote by A. W. Tozer who wrote, "Whoever defends himself will have himself for his defense, and he will have no other. But let him become defenseless before the Lord and he will have for his defender no less than

God Himself." When my 30-day deadline had concluded, I was instructed to go directly to the administrator's office the following morning where he would advise me of my status. My assistant clocked out and had just left so I was alone in the warehouse. I walked over to my desk to get my car keys when I heard the Lord say, "Gather all of your things and clean out your desk because you're not coming back here."

As expected, the following morning I was advised that my continued employment with the county was over unless I could counter with a valid argument. He laid down a single piece of typing paper and slid it across the table to me, then handed me a ballpoint pen and said, "You're welcome to write down anything said here today that you don't agree with by way of your defense which we will consider before we finalize our decision." I looked at the paper lying in front of me and slid it back across the table and said, "I have nothing to write down because regardless of what I put on that paper you've already made your decision." I left the building and made my way over to a separate county building where Krys' office was located. I walked in the door, went up to her desk and said, "Dear, I just got fired. Let's celebrate! Lunch is on me."

It was quite unsettling to be fired in that manner, but I sensed there was a purpose involved—although it lacked clarity in that moment. A few weeks later, things were brought into enough focus for me to realize that losing my job served as both the catalyst and the tailwind that put us on track to finding an authentic story I'd been searching for. Ironically, it ended up starting with us. In retrospect, I realized something I hadn't before considered—our lives become a story, and I didn't need to go searching for one.

Six months after I was fired, Krys and I arrived on the mission field.

6.

To the Field

One of our liabilities as Christians is the tendency to use a litmus test and refuse to move forward unless we see a green light. Krys and I didn't have a definitive green light indicating we were to move to the mission field. Rather, we believed it was something worth pursuing and the loss of my job seemed to provide an opportunity, so we began looking into the mechanics of how that might happen. The obvious first step was to discuss it with the leadership of our home church, New Song Church, and inquire if they would prayerfully consider sending us out as missionaries.

We proposed that we would just try it out for a year before deciding if we wanted to extend. It seemed like a fairly safe plan with no long-term commitment from us or the church. After a lengthy meeting, Pastor Richard Probasco and the elders agreed to send us to the mission field as their first official missionaries. They offered to pay for our plane tickets and committed to $400 per month in financial support. Krys and I were overjoyed at such an offer, which we felt was incredibly gracious.

We looked at one small mission sending organization based in Washington State to serve as a covering for us, but when I inquired about joining, it seemed they were more interested in the 20% administrative fee they would deduct from whatever money we raised—rather than showing interest in what we would be doing as their potential missionaries. When I expressed my shock at the fee they lowered it, as if it was a negotiable term. And, the more I hesitated the lower the fee went. I guess that turned me off to pursuing other organizations. Thankfully, the church offered to step in and serve as our sending agency, meaning they processed donations and provided any additional logistical support we needed.

Bruce Olson related a story in his book *Bruchko* about fellow missionaries who ostracized him when they learned he wasn't sent out by an established mission organization. He just got on a plane and went to the mission field because he felt compelled to serve the Motilone Indians of Columbia, South America.

We've met countless missionaries serving with various mission organizations over the years, but I didn't know that joining a mission organization was the preferred or recommended way to go to the mission field. I suppose our small hometown experiences sent Krys and I into the world with a predetermined value system regarding self-reliance. I'll admit this mentality has presented both pros and cons over the years. Large established organizations, for example, provide extensive member care and administrative support such as assistance with securing the appropriate visas, while we just did it all on our own.

We arrived in the Philippines four months later with less than $800 per month in committed financial support and $2,000 of our own personal money in the bank. I learned later that most missionaries were required to raise a minimum of $3,000 monthly at the time. We were so naive and lacked any depth of understanding concerning the amount of adequate funding needed to function, but we were committed. Thankfully, God providentially provided and connected us with a missionary couple who were searching for someone to house-sit for them while they took a one-year furlough. Their house was situated on a hilltop on the outskirts of Manila, which provided a spectacular view of the expansive mega-city teeming with 15 million residents.

* * *

Faith Academy, one of the world's largest and best known schools for missionary kids, was located near the house where we were staying. The school was by default a central location for a growing missionary community due to the fact that many missionaries had their children enrolled in the school. Within a few weeks of our arrival, we had met dozens of missionaries representing all sorts of mission organizations and found that several went out of their way to welcome new missionaries to the field. People would often drop by to say "hello" and ask how we were doing and offer to help in any way. We were honored and listened intently and carefully as they shared their stories, trusting they were obviously qualified experts compared to our lack of experience.

I found that several of them liked to talk about their respective ministries, and some tended to lean a bit much on the narcissistic side of the spectrum. We noticed a contrast between short and long term missionaries which I've often observed over the years. Those who've been on the field five years or less seem a bit more excited and vocal about sharing what God was doing in their ministries. The old timers—those who had been on the field ten-plus years—are quite a bit more reserved, having developed a keener understanding of the complexities of living cross culturally, and take more time to seek the Lord based on wisdom gained through extensive experience.

I began to better understand this after Krys and I reached our 10-year mark as well. Not all, but many new missionaries seem to tackle too many things at once and spread themselves out too thin, which can limit the attention and oversight a primary project or ministry needs. The mission field presents itself with a multitude of opportunities, but a lack of discretion and experience prevent new missionaries from stepping away from some of those opportunities. I've also witnessed that many newly arrived missionaries are not teachable to some extent, which may be the result of passion and excitement. I can certainly empathize with that passion. One of the important lessons I've learned over the past 20+ years is simply this; just because an opportunity is presented it doesn't necessarily mean God is in it. Opportunities are definitely assured, but fruit isn't. I've watch many people leave the field because they never found a place to drive their stake into the ground and commit to one or two things—or they were more inclined to go after the low hanging fruit. Once that fruit is gathered they lacked the tenacity, patience, fortitude and prayer commitment to work for the harder to reach fruit at the top of the tree, which may take years of cultivation until the harvest is ready.

Within a week of our arrival, one of the longer serving missionaries stopped by and introduced himself. Mike was genuinely friendly with a gentle disposition, and during our brief visit he asked a few questions about our plans for ministry. I told him we wanted to help serve the local churches with discipleship training, but we had no idea exactly how that was going to look.

Mike then said something I thought was a bit unusual, but it got my attention. He said, "Don't be surprised if you discover that God has something entirely different planned than what you were expecting." I had no idea at the time just how right he was. God did have a completely different plan for our lives, which began to unfold a few days later.

* * *

Krys and I were waiting for the house-sitting arrangement to begin when the couple was scheduled to depart for the U.S. the following month. In the meantime, prior to our arrival in the Philippines we had been referred to another Manila-based missionary family by the pastor of Krys' home church in Idaho, which was part of an affiliation of small independent churches scattered around northern Idaho, western Montana and western Canada. This family's home church was also a member of this affiliation, thus the connection. Initially, we planned to partner with them and we were temporarily staying in their guest bedroom until we could move into the other house. The husband was a former Army Special Forces medic and his wife was a teacher. They had been on the field for about six years, and the house they rented was a split-level home that had a room on the ground level with a separate entrance, which they had turned into a small medical clinic.

Occasionally, local women from a nearby squatter community would come and deliver their babies because they couldn't afford hospital fees. We'd been there about two weeks when one of the Filipino midwives, whom this missionary couple had hired, came upstairs where Krys and I were working on our very first newsletter. She invited Krys to come downstairs and watch the birth of a baby, but Krys graciously declined.

Fifteen minutes later, the midwife came upstairs a second time to invite Krys to watch the birth. Again, Krys respectfully declined because she had no interest in such a thing.

The midwife reappeared once again about ten minutes later and politely asked Krys to please come downstairs. Sensing Krys' apprehension she assured her it would be OK and suggested that she could just stand in the background and watch. At this point I elbowed Krys and told her it was time to surrender, which she did and followed the midwife downstairs.

About 45 minutes later I heard Krys walk back upstairs, but I didn't look at her directly until she whispered, "Look what I have." I turned and saw a new baby in her arms that might have been all of 15 minutes old. I briefly glanced at the baby then looked at Krys, who was glowing.

Mark Twain once said, "The two most important dates in your life is the day you were born and the day you find out why." The expression on my wife's face looked like she'd just had a glimpse of why God put her on planet earth. At that moment, I could see that Krys was called to be a midwife, but not just any midwife. Looking back on that time, 25 years ago, I wonder if God stirred the heart of that young Filipino midwife to be so respectfully insistent in inviting Krys to join her in witnessing the birth of that baby.

Beginning with that single encounter, God led us to start a ministry that literally touched tens of thousands of lives and trained over two hundred missionaries—some of whom have gone on to serve in 15 foreign countries.

7

Laying the Groundwork

Robyn and Mark were the missionary couple who had invited us to house-sit for them. They were professional artists who cultivated relationships with Manila's national artists and several people from the business community, including wealthy patrons who supported the arts. Over time they were able to build an extensive network, which enabled them to share the plight of street prostitutes in Ermita—the shady red light district of Manila. Donations were gathered from this network and used to help reach prostitutes and secure ways to rescue them from a lifestyle they felt powerless to escape.

Robyn and Mark planned to be on furlough for 12 months and preferred to have someone take care of their house rather than giving it up, leaving them no place to store their furniture. It was a perfect arrangement because they offered to cover the rent if we'd commit to paying the utilities. It didn't take us long to become settled in a place to call home after we moved in.

We considered working with the missionary who initially hosted us in his home and had the clinic in his basement, but it wasn't a good fit because he was a bit too intense for us. We had, however, been introduced to Frank and Liz Amantea who were missionaries from Canada. They lived in a house about a mile from where we were staying and their three children attended Faith Academy. Like us, they arrived on the mission field as independent missionaries the year before we arrived. Liz was volunteering at Faith and Frank had been serving in various capacities as a teacher or guest speaker in various national churches and a small local bible school.

Frank and Liz are incredibly gracious people, and they sort of adopted us as young missionaries new to the field by helping us get settled and inviting us to become part of their family. About 10 years separated our ages, but the relationship they cultivated with Krys and me led us to realize years later that their integrity, obedience to God, and investment in our lives was one of the main reasons we became successful as career missionaries.

Frank had sensed for some time that God wanted him to plant a new church and invited me to be involved if I was interested. I was honored, although I had no idea what I could do to help him start a new church. I was intrigued with Frank's faith and tenacity to just walk things out day-by-day and step-by-step. We started holding mini-crusades in the basketball courts of the surrounding barrios (*barangays*) by showing *The Jesus Movie* followed with an exhortation. People responded, so it was rewarding. Initially Frank was content to open his home as a venue for the new church, but one day he noticed an old boarded-up building located on Ortigas Avenue, which is the main road going into Manila. It had been a disco bar, which the owner shut down after she learned the tenant started offering customers a bit more than dancing in the dimly lit rooms located behind the kitchen. Frank sought her out and we were shocked when she offered him the use of her building rent free when he confided his plan was to use it for a new church. We thought she may have been inclined to feel that allowing a church to meet there was in some way redemptive after learning about all the sin that had been sponsored in her building.

One of the things I genuinely appreciated about Frank is he had no pretenses about promoting himself or the church. He was just obeying God and trusting the Lord would add to our numbers. I once asked someone who their target group was and he replied, "People." Frank didn't really have a defined target group because we were reaching out to the middle class as well as the poor. Middle class businessmen were worshiping God during Sunday services standing next to poor men who lived each day scratching out ways to take care of their families.

The church grew slowly but steadily. It was a collection of people just wanting to serve God and learn how to use their spiritual gifts. We also started a resident bible school with an enrollment of about a dozen young people fresh out of high school. The tuition was free, but we asked each student to pay what they could to help cover the cost to feed them. It was informal and we ran it more like a *school of the local church*, teaching people how to share the gospel and be involved in the church. One day each week was set aside for evangelism and we'd take the students out to visit homes and share the gospel with anyone willing to listen. God used that to grow the church.

* * *

In the meantime, Krys pursued avenues involving midwifery as a result of watching the birth of that baby. She was introduced to another missionary, Jeri Gunderson, who lived in the foothills near Antipolo at the outlying edge of Manila, about three miles from our house. Jeri was a lay midwife, and with the support of her husband they transformed their home into a clinic serving impoverished women living in nearby squatter areas. Jeri had hired a few Filipino midwives and it was rare to visit their house and not see several pregnant women waiting in the living room for a prenatal exam or delivering their baby in a back bedroom which had been converted into a delivery room. Krys and Jeri hit it off immediately because they were both from Montana.

It didn't take long for Jeri to ask Krys if she would be interested in volunteering at her clinic. Initially, Krys was taught how to do prenatal exams and watched a few deliveries, which led to more hands-on involvement in the birth room. Eventually Krys was apprenticing under Jeri and her daughter, Deborah, as well as the Filipino midwives serving on staff. The experience served as a practical training model for Krys because it provided direct supervision from a competent and skilled person.

Krys also had an opportunity to serve at another missionary-based clinic managed by Denie Hepner located on the other side of Manila, which meant she could be on call at either clinic. I remember racing her to either one of those clinics countless times on my motorcycle in the middle of the night.

Over time, Krys was becoming proficient with the protocols and procedures, which enabled her to recognize the signs of pre-eclampsia during a prenatal exam or manage a hemorrhage during labor and delivery. Within a couple of years her skill level, for the most part, was on a par with those of a professional midwife.

The validity of a skilled missionary midwife serving in a cross-cultural context was becoming more and more evident to us, which is primarily due to the favor a midwife gains with a woman and her family. We began to integrate Krys' growing midwifery skills into our ministry, which was certainly not something we had considered upon our arrival to the field. Eventually, an idea was proposed to merge maternal healthcare with the church planting efforts. Krys and Liz, who is a nurse, hosted a prenatal clinic inside the church building every Wednesday and invited impoverished women from a nearby squatter area to come for free care. It provided a new avenue to reach people with the gospel message, and we began to notice the favor Krys and Liz gained from their patients was different than what we witnessed at other evangelistic outreaches. That favor naturally spilled over and influenced the husbands of the patients, a few of whom started attending the church.

Krys and I were on a vast learning curve as new missionaries. A typical mission strategy is to go into a new area and look for a "person of peace" who is someone influential in the community. Then, if everything goes as planned, they will invite you to share with their *oikos* web of extended relationships. We realized in the years following that a Christian midwife can serve by proxy as that person of peace. The community embraces her skills and defers many health care issues to her, especially in the remote provincial areas lacking professional medical practitioners—thus enabling her to become a person of peace in the community. Furthermore, a midwife enters into a long-term relationship with her patients, which naturally influences the external families of both the patient and her husband (*bana*).

The words of that missionary who suggested God might have something different for us started coming to fruition. As it turned out, what was happening with Krys was the initial planting of seeds that would go on to define our ministry work in the years to come, and eventually produce a harvest we hadn't expected.

8.

Aetas

Krys and I were alternating our time between Manila and building a relationship with a young national pastor, Joey Lacap, whom I had met during my first visit to the Philippines back in 1988. He had pioneered two new church plants in Balanga City—the provincial capital of Bataan—located about three hours by bus from Manila on the opposite side of Manila Bay. I was thrilled to reconnect with Joey and his wife, Beth, and introduce them to Krys. They were delighted to see that I had returned with my new wife to serve in the Philippines as a missionary couple.

Joey had a definite teaching gift and was very good expounding on scripture during his sermons, but he was quite reserved and introverted, preferring to study in the privacy of his room most of the day. His wife, Beth, on the other hand, represented the heart of the ministry. She was relationally oriented and had tremendous favor with everyone she came in contact with, whether it was a street vendor or a government official. They were a young couple, about our age, and very sincere and eager to serve the Lord in ministry. Both were honored to have us partner with them, but we were very careful to just serve and build relationships without acting like we had all the answers.

Every other week, Krys and I would travel by jeepney and bus to Bataan to spend a week serving in the Lacap's church that numbered about 50 people, which according to published statistics is the average size of a Filipino church. The church members were loving people and we felt accepted as part of their church body. We never expected any special favoritism, nor did they approach us with underlying motives such as seeking financial help. Pastor Joey and his family were incredibly gracious in allowing us to stay in their home, which is typical of the hospitable culture

Filipinos are known for. It was with them that I learned to be prepared in season and out of season because we were often taken to a bible study unannounced and told we were leading it.

One day, Pastor Joey and Beth invited us to accompany them to a small community up in the mountains where they had pioneered a new outreach ministry, which was an extension of their church. We rode in the passenger cabin of a motorcycle combination tricycle, known as a *trisikad*, as the driver maneuvered along a narrow-rutted dirt road that got worse the higher we traveled and eventually ended at a large open clearing. Situated on a grassy bluff at the base of the mountain were several bamboo huts and dark-skinned people, some of whom were sitting down while others seemed to be preoccupied with a chore or taking care of their children. A group of men were off to the side chopping something with their sharp machetes (*bolos*).

Krys and I felt like we had stepped into the pages of a National Geographic magazine as we made our way toward the huts, closely following behind Joey and Beth. The villagers were Aborigines, whom we later learned were indigenous natives. Joey and Beth initially identified them as "Negritos"— a term carried over from the Spanish colonial era, but they are more commonly referred to as Aetas (pronounced EYE-tas). The adults were between 4' and 5' tall, with black curly hair and looked of a lineage different than typical Filipinos of Malay descent. All of them were thin, and not particularly muscular. Their feet were wide, due to lack of shoes, and thickly calloused. They were dressed in shorts which had holes in them and were generally two sizes too large with a woven grass string through the belt loops. They also wore stained t-shirts and a few had rubber sandals, but most were barefoot.

The village layout lacked any arrangement; with huts randomly erected at various places along a red-colored dirt pathway that stretched about 500 meters through the center of their village, upwards toward where the mountain began its more vertical ascent. Each hut was relatively well built with long thick branches serving as the main corner posts that had been pushed vertically down into the ground about one foot. Tied to them were smaller branches positioned laterally that held *sawali*—a durable woven matting made from split bamboo and used as stiff walling material. The roofs were made of species of palm leaves called *nipa* or long bundled grass called *cogon,* which has dense stalks and is quite strong and durable. Cogan grows in abundance throughout the country and the Aetas sometimes use it to make handicrafts such as native baskets, small purses and various decorative things. It can also be processed and formed into paper once it's chopped up and the cellular material is broken down using caustic acid. Sheets of paper are formed when a wood-framed deckle is immersed into water containing the slurry or pulpy material, and pulled out to drain and then dried after being transferred to a drying table. The Aeta people harvest and bundle the grass and transport it to the marketplaces in the lowlands where a wholesaler pays them for the entire load. Pastor Joey explained that their livelihood primarily revolved around gathering and selling the grass, growing papaya, bananas and root crops—mostly sweet potatoes or *kamote,* which they pound with a large wooden mortar and pestle to break down the fiber for consumption.

A typical hut (*bahay kubo*) was sparsely furnished and contained a rough bed and table made from bamboo and one or two aluminum pots sitting next to a small area on one side of the hut where a fire was used to cook their food. Clothes were kept in an old cardboard box or a handmade basket woven from bamboo splits. The inside of each hut was dirty and smelled like damp earth mixed with rotting thatch and the pungent odor of the smoke-blackened ceiling caused by the cooking fire.

The Aetas were thought to have migrated from Australia centuries ago and are considered to be among the first original inhabitants of the Philippines. Traditionally a hunting/gathering people, the Aetas were well experienced in jungle survival and some were hired during the Vietnam War to teach the U.S. Military special-forces transitioning through the naval base at Subic Bay about jungle survival skills known as JEST (Jungle Escape Survival Training).

Pastor Joey explained that these particular Aetas were refugees from Mt. Pinatubo after it erupted in 1991 and destroyed many of their villages. Scientists claim it was the second-largest volcanic eruption of this century and ten times larger than the 1980 eruption of Mount St. Helens in Washington State. They had been evacuated by the military in helicopters to this area where they erected huts on a tract of land the government had set aside for them.

I clearly remember, as if I was looking at a photograph pulled from my wallet, the images imprinted on my mind from when we first walked into that village. On a sloping ridge, just a short distance to the north of the village was a national shrine and a 90-meter-high cross erected in memory of the American and Filipino forces who surrendered to the Japanese during World War II. To the east, you can clearly see Corregidor Island (*Isla ng Corregidor*) sitting at the entrance of Manila Bay, which the U.S. military had fortified as a harbor defense. General Douglas MacArthur used Corregidor as his headquarters until he was forced to abandon it prior to the Japanese winning control of the Bataan Peninsula. Today it serves as a historic monument visited by thousands of tourists each year.

The Aeta village was situated in the exact location where thousands of American and Filipino men had dug themselves in—as a last ditch defensive stronghold against the Japanese—who effectively overcame any hope of escape during the siege of Bataan. After three months of heavy fighting, 74,000 weak, sick and wounded U.S. and Filipino forces finally surrendered and were subjected to the brutal Bataan Death March where more than 20,000 soldiers perished due to the horrors and brutality they endured by the Japanese who forced them to walk 97 kilometers to the prison camps set up in Tarlac, Pampanga. During the march, the Japanese showed no mercy. The American and Filipino prisoners were starved and given no water. When a solider collapsed along the road, they were shot or bayoneted on the spot.

The entire area we were standing on was rich in World War II history, and the Aetas showed us many things they'd found such as knives, bayonets, bullet shells, and canteen remnants from the military. I was enthralled looking at those various artifacts as we held their history in our hands, knowing each piece undoubtedly had a tale of death, horror and suffering to tell.

* * *

Pastor Joey and Beth had prayerfully decided their church would establish an outreach ministry in the village and invited us to partner with them. We intentionally did our best to stay in the background and let them take the lead in whatever they felt led to do. As an initial step, the church leadership decided to help provide some basic education classes in the village twice a week, and we were pleased to see their commitment went beyond just talking about it. After several months, we asked if it would be helpful to raise enough funds to build a small concrete building, enabling the school to transition into a more formal setting instead of meeting under a large mango tree.

Pastor Joey thought it was a good idea and the village chief also agreed. However, we were a bit taken aback when the village elders informed us that none of the Aetas would help with the project. I thought surely I had missed something in the cultural nuances that tend to cause well-intentioned plans to go awry. However, we later learned the villagers had valid reasons to be skeptical. Other people—primarily government officials—had apparently offered assistance in the past but never honored their word, so the villagers had a hard time believing outsiders and therefore wouldn't commit to helping. We understood and made the decision to move forward.

As we began the project there was one particular logistical problem, which became a back breaking and physically exhausting challenge. We decided to build the school walls and floor using concrete rather than wood, which the termites would have destroyed. While this made perfect sense, the only water source was a shallow stream situated at the bottom of a ravine located beside the village. We were hosting a short-term team from our home church who had come to assist us with the project and I drew the short straw to help fetch the water using plastic containers. We'd hike down to the stream, fill the containers and then hoist them on our shoulders, packing them back up the hill, and dump the water into an old 55 gallon steel drum until we needed it for mixing the concrete. It only took one trip to realize the gravity of the challenge we faced.

I was exhausted after three trips hauling water out of that ravine, and the Aeta men—who were gathered in a group tying bundles of cogan grass—refused to offer any assistance even though it was entirely evident we were struggling with the chore. Much to the surprise of one of the short-term

Americans who was helping me, I decided to confront the men using some dramatic flair. I yelled to get their attention, and as they curiously faced me I unscrewed the cap off the five-gallon plastic jug full of water, which I'd just lugged up the hill, and proceeded to pour the contents out on the ground in front of them. For added dramatic effect I shook out the extra drops of water then tossed the empty container at their feet—an act I fully intended to serve as an indictment of their apathy.

When missionaries try something new, it will generally go in one of two directions. Either it works out as he hoped or it goes sideways if he doesn't take the time to think before diving in head first. If the Aetas wanted an education for their children then they were going to participate, and in that particular moment I felt compelled to punch through their dismissive attitude regardless of whether it was rooted in their culture or not. I wanted the village to take responsibility with the project and be involved in what we were doing for their children rather than viewing it as a free handout.

There was a long pause as everyone processed what I'd just done, but what happened next was absolutely unexpected. The village women who had been sitting to the side watching the entire situation unfold as first-hand witnesses suddenly came alive, like someone had flipped on a switch. No longer were they passive observers because once they connected the dots—and understood the inference I'd made—they immediately stole the spotlight and became the main characters. I never could have anticipated what unfolded next.

The women became furious and animated and started shouting and pointing their fingers at those men who were their husbands, sons and brothers. At first I didn't understand what was happening because I assumed their shouts were directed at me, but then I realized they were scolding the men and yelling at them to get down that hill and help carry water!

Those men had been handed their pride on a bamboo platter by a bunch of women, which made it even more humiliating. They immediately moved without any hesitation or argument, and within 20 minutes we had all the water we needed. In fact, every day afterward, when we arrived in the village to continue our work we found the steel drum and all the plastic containers full of water. We never again needed to make another trek down the ravine.

———————————

We and the visitors from our home church had "invaded" the Aeta village. However, the Aetas—unknown to anyone at the time—were about to "invade" the United States.

Before that could happen, though, I needed to figure out a missiological strategy and ask the Aeta men a bunch of questions.

9.

Greenhorns

At this point, Krys and I were, for all intents and purposes, greenhorn missionaries lacking any depth of missiological understanding aside from having hearts that just wanted to help people. Being new to the mission field is similar to being lost in the mountains without a map or compass. We look for a place to get our bearings but can't, so we wander around until it gets dark, then realize we didn't bring supplies to spend the night in the woods. We're lonely, scared, cold, tired and hungry. Understanding the culture at a depth necessary to be effective is vague at best. There are language barriers and things happen that we're unable to understand at the outset because we filter everything through our own culture.

One day I'm taking inventory at my warehouse job in Portland then six months later I'm on the other side of the planet, walking into the pages of a National Geographic magazine. My cumulative experience working with tribal people in a relatively short amount of time was hosting a village water fight with a bunch of five-foot-tall curly-haired men while their wives and mothers served as my cheerleaders. I was about as equipped for this task as a diesel mechanic pretending to be a Starbucks barista, standing in front of a $20,000 Mastrena espresso machine while trying to make sense of a customer's order; "*Grande, iced, non-fat, upside down, double pump, caramel Macchiato,*" when his entire coffee experience is limited to drinking cheap black Robusta from a greasy Styrofoam cup back in his shop. He thinks a Macchiato is an expensive Italian sports car, and asks his co-worker to get the mop ready because the customer wants it served upside down.

Krys and I were just like that mechanic. We had no idea what we were doing but we wanted to learn, and we genuinely wanted to serve the Filipino people.

I once had the opportunity to tour a silver mine in Montana. We were eventually brought into a large milling room where two enormous ball mills were spinning in opposing unison to each other. The amount of crushing force it took for these huge machines to pulverize house-sized pieces of solid rock brought out of the mountain was amazing to watch. The phenomenal amount of energy and millions of dollars spent in machinery, fuel, engineering, and the manpower it takes to process massive tons of rock just to find a single ounce of silver was impressive. Missionaries will likewise spend a lot of time and prayer and energy seeking the best way to bring the gospel to people—often with minimal results for the amount of labor expended. We make mistakes, and try and try again and again, prayerfully struggling to see fruit from the seed we're sowing. Missionaries will hear about an idea or a strategy then unpack and study it and look at it from every conceivable angle to see if any part of it might be applicable to our work.

At that time, we'd only been on the field for about six months and neither of us had any training to be missionaries. The only resource I had was the 900-page three-inch-thick *Perspectives on the World Christian Movement Reader* I borrowed from another missionary, which I read cover-to-cover. It was the go-to bible for missionaries before the Internet. Today, missionaries have immediate access to a multitude of mission related articles, books, strategies, resources and materials that can easily be downloaded to help their ministries. We didn't have access to any of those things and were, therefore, amateurs at best. Maybe having the *Perspectives* book as a reference had somewhat qualified us to be missionaries, but reading a book is no substitute for actual experience in the field.

The following story explains the difference. I used to serve as a technical director for a mobile production company that traveled extensively around the States. We had a large truck full of theatrical equipment, which included portable staging, theatrical lights, trusses, sound system, cable, and pyrotechnic equipment. We were in the process of setting up in a large open-air field at UNLV's campus in Las Vegas and needed a primary electrical source to power our equipment. There was a frat house adjacent to the field so we approached the guys living there and inquired if we could tap into their electrical box.

They agreed and as I was tapping into a breaker someone came up behind me. His tone resonated with a kind of questioning defiance as he asked, "What the (bad word) are you doing?" He claimed to be the frat house president and hadn't been advised that we'd already received permission from his fellow frat brothers to tap their electricity. He seemed O.K. with that once I updated him, but then he started challenging me, claiming he was a fourth-year electrical engineering student and demanded to know if I was qualified to tap into the breakers. I assured him that I knew exactly what I was doing. He became agitated and claimed I wasn't qualified compared to him, so I asked if he'd ever tapped into a main panel before to which he replied he had not. I was a bit facetious and said, "So, you're a 4th year electrical engineering student and you've never done something as basic as tapping into a breaker panel? All you have is a bunch of book knowledge but no actual experience. Whereas I may not have the book knowledge like you do, but I've done this many times. So, who's more qualified?" He turned around and walked away.

Cross-cultural foreign missions are a bit like that story. Experience doesn't always trump knowledge, but I've seen many times that regardless of how much studying we undertake, it will never bear fruit until we get our hands dirty and immerse ourselves into the work and tap into the breaker. My grandfather helped me understand that truth when he assured me that I could fix my car even though I wasn't a mechanic.

I used to own a 1972 Buick sedan and the rear main seal developed a significant leak, but I didn't have the money to take it to a professional mechanic. My grandpa, who was a self-taught engineer without a high school education, encouraged me to fix it myself using the tools he had at his house, but I felt the job was beyond my ability. He said, "You'll figure it out if you just try." It took me 10 hours to replace that seal—only to discover I didn't do it right, so I had to tear it apart and do it all over again. Although it took a long time, I ended up saving a few hundred dollars.

Read any missionary book and you will see a common thread woven throughout their stories—we're trying to figure things out. But, we're doing it prayerfully. Admittedly, it comes with frustration, discouragement and disappointment, but we continue with a sense of fortitude who "spends himself in a worthy cause... and who at the worst, if he fails, at least fails while trying" as Teddy Roosevelt said.

* * *

The guy from our home church who was visiting from the States and observed my confrontation with the Aetas may have thought I really outsmarted those men—but I hadn't. The response from the village women was only natural and they'd have done the same thing if the circumstances, situation or another person had done what I did. It took me a while to understand that so much of the fruitfulness in ministry is based on relationships. If I had taken the time or understood the value of cultivating relationships before attempting to build a school, which in retrospect we pursued much too prematurely, it would have served us and the Aetas much better.

All of the sights, smells, and sounds we as foreigners experience when we visit other countries are fascinating, but what we don't understand are the value systems, worldviews and the process of how people in other cultures think. True understanding and empathy comes only through relationship, which cultivates the soil and prepares it to respond to the seed planted. The people in the Asian country where I serve are relationally oriented, unlike people in the west where we often allow time and events to take precedence over everything else. The purpose driven value I had prioritized in my mind was to build the school. Sometimes we forget to lay aside an agenda or project and simply cultivate relationships, realizing that we could mutually learn from each other. Yes, it's true that we asked the Aetas if they were interested in building the church/school to which they said "Yes," but the more I began to understand the culture the more I realized that a negative reply to a question is not culturally appropriate, even if that is what they want to say. They were saying "Yes" to the idea, but as Westerners we were focused on the project rather than the people. In other words, the building became the issue rather than the people who would benefit from it.

I really misunderstood much in the cultural communication styles initially, but as time and years went by I learned that Westerners view so many things as right or wrong, black or white, yes or no. The standard by which our western interpreted positions are held or judgments made lack a larger context of understanding and, unfortunately, we fail to provide enough room for personal honor, which is an important cultural value.

I once asked someone to do something for me, but they judged my outward actions rather than judging my heart, assuming what I was requesting was wrong and sinful. They accused me of being unrighteous and challenged my integrity. I have found in this culture that people are incredibly expansive in grace to overlook a sin that someone else committed, more so than when someone challenges their integrity—resulting in dishonor to the other person.

I have been just as guilty in judging issues and situations while serving as a missionary. Filipinos have what's called "kinship groups," in which people find their identity and value within the respective groups to which they belong. Value is placed on togetherness rather than being independent and individualistic. Roles and decisions are made by the group, and as foreigners we are generally outside of the kinship group until we take the time to cultivate relationships.

* * *

I've watched many new missionaries arrive on the field front-loaded— meaning their understanding of the mission field was unevenly distributed. I once recalled listening in shock to a new missionary publicly state that he didn't need a cultural orientation and challenged the person who was leading the orientation. Krys and I both understood that we didn't know what we were doing when we arrived on the field and we admitted it. Oftentimes I would default back to Ephesians 4 where Paul says in verses 10–12 that the five-fold ministry gifts are given to equip the saints for the work of the ministry. I felt that our job as missionaries wasn't to do the work of the ministry ourselves, but rather to help empower and equip the nationals and let them take it to the forefront.

Years later, as our understanding matured, we let our senior Filipino staff take an expansive role by encouraging them be the face of our mission organization—particularly regarding the need to interact with multiple government agencies because they excel at understanding both the undertones and breadth of the cultural nuances we as foreigners often miss. Initially, that level of empowerment was difficult for them to accept because the culture is hierarchical, and employees, who are under authority, are reluctant to engage themselves on the level that empowerment is designed to enable. It took years of cultivating our trust in them to see its benefits.

Thankfully we continued to see God's grace cover so many shortcomings on our part. We genuinely wanted to serve the national church and help them minister to the villagers, but the outreach to the village was also a new endeavor for Pastor Joey and Beth. They were doing their best working with the Aetas, trying to navigate the unfamiliar culture they presented to Joey and Beth as Filipinos.

* * *

Krys and I have witnessed many times over the past years that healthcare can play an important role in opening the doors for the gospel message. Something interesting occurred that we hadn't expected, which led to a key turning point in our ministry amongst the Aetas. Krys had been studying primary healthcare in David Werner's book *Where There is No Doctor*, which became an excellent resource for treating many of the children in the village who suffered from common flus and various skin diseases. A major underlying problem that adversely affects the health of children in developing countries is malnutrition. Most Aetas suffered from protein deficiency because sources of animal protein are scarce. Livestock is not raised and I may have counted three chickens running loose around the village. Occasionally the men hunted for wild boar in the mountains. There were no gardens in the village other than a small area planted with cassava, which is a starchy root they would eat in addition to wild mango and papaya.

As we were departing the village one day, an Aeta woman approached Krys and held up her baby, which was suffering from a severe case of impetigo—an infectious skin disease caused by a bacterial infection. The baby's forehead and the area around its mouth was covered with inflamed blisters. Krys entrusted some money to one of Pastor Joey's church members who accompanied us and advised her to buy Gentian Violet and antibacterial soap at a local pharmacy down in the town proper, then explained how to treat the infection.

For some reason we were unable to return to the village for several weeks, but Beth reported later that the GV and soap had cleared up the impetigo. However, something else had occurred. Beth confided the successful treatment of that baby was the catalyst that helped us gain additional favor with the Aetas. This prompted Krys to host several primary healthcare clinics in the village where she treated various ailments as guided by her reference book, which didn't require a medical degree.

* * *

The simple one-room school building was finally completed. A member from Pastor Joey's church committed to travel up to the village twice each week where she taught the Aeta children, starting with the basics. The school and healthcare we provided played a significant role in helping break down walls of resistance in the community to the extent that one of the Aeta families offered their hut for us to use whenever we visited the village. They had recently vacated it and moved into a new hut they'd built.

At one point, we decided to show *The Jesus Movie* using a small generator and a portable movie projector. We discretely laughed when some of the villagers walked behind a large sheet, which served as an improvised movie screen suspended between two trees. They couldn't comprehend how the images moved on the sheet and were attempting to see where the actors were behind the screen. Actually, we tried to show the movie on three separate occasions, with each attempt failing due to technical problems with the sound. Eventually, one of the church members offered to narrate the entire film from memory because he had seen it several times. It was hard to discern what the Aetas were thinking as they watched the movie, and I was unsettled about the whole thing because I felt they lacked sufficient context.

The Aetas spoke a dialect known as Kapampangan and we came up short looking for any materials to help reach them with the gospel. I'd heard about a strategy developed by Trevor McIlwain who published a series of manuals called *Building on Firm Foundations*. His approach focuses on teaching through the Old Testament chronologically while carefully highlighting the plan of redemption God revealed in so many of the stories, which pointed to the revealing of His Son. Most bible studies are non-sequential and use isolated scriptures, but we understood that Filipino people love stories and they needed to process them amongst a larger context aside from isolated verses. Most tribal people have an animistic concept of God or a creator, and their lack of biblical context causes them to become lost before a typical western-style bible study even begins. "Jesus loves you and has a wonderful plan for your life" means nothing to an Aeta. Don Richardson carefully points out in his book *Eternity in Their Heart* that God has not left Himself without a witness (Acts 14), and His witness among tribal people can become evident by asking them basic questions about creation and their lives respective of a creator.

My favorite verse in the entire bible is John 17:3 which records a portion of Jesus' lengthy prayer which I feel is the crown jewel of what he prayed in the Garden of Gethsemane. I once shared with a group of people during a bible study that if God was to reach down from heaven and point to a single verse in the bible, which summed up everything, it would be this particular verse. It might have been a stretch to make such a claim, but the emphasis I wanted to highlight is as the verse says. "And this is eternal life, that they may know you the only true God and Jesus Christ whom you have sent." The whole purpose of eternal life is to *know* God and his Son, Jesus.

Although the context and meaning of that verse is easily understood by a western Christian, a tribal person lacks the ability to understand, having no context or history by which to comprehend or grasp what is being communicated. God's character and His purpose are revealed in the history of the bible, and Jesus was the fulfillment of Old Testament prophecies and the redemptive plan of God. The context of the gospel as explained to tribal people isn't contained in "four spiritual laws," or in an evangelistic crusade, or showing *The Jesus Movie*. The objective is to connect God's redemptive plan revealed in Old Testament history to the person of God's son whom He later sent to become the promised Redeemer.

I was able to secure McIlwain's materials and spent days studying them. Although, admittedly, I was a rookie missionary, I thought McIlwain's approach to reaching tribal people was the best and only option we had to guide our approach in evangelizing the Aeta people in that village. One particular emphasis described in the strategy, which made complete sense, although I'd never considered it, was the need to prepare people to hear the gospel before presenting it. Because the Aetas are animistic we asked a series of questions that were specifically designed to be respectful of their religious beliefs and culture, then use that as a launching point to get them to consider things beyond what they believed spiritually. The objective was to subtly plant a small seed of doubt in their hearts, which simply involved asking how they knew their answers to our questions were true. It was an entirely non-threatening and respectful way to help establish the authority of the bible for tribal people before the gospel would be presented.

It was really important for me to make sure Pastor Joey felt comfortable with this, and I took the time to explain it thoroughly and let him study the materials. I again felt that my role as a missionary was to honor Ephesians 4 and help equip others to do the work of the ministry. When Joey affirmed his support for the strategy I knew he wasn't just accommodating me as the foreign missionary. He fully understood that he too was acting in the role of a missionary trying to reach this village with the gospel message.

During our next visit, Joey and I approached the Aeta chief and respectfully asked if he would be willing to gather the men in order to participate in a survey. He agreed and a time was set to meet later in the week. An old mango tree—known as a century tree—with a massive trunk supporting a wide canopy sat at the entrance of the village. Its expansive network of branches and leaves easily provided enough shade to serve as our venue. The meeting was called, and sitting down on the exposed roots of that tree with the village elders sitting on their haunches in a large circle is an image I'll never forget. I began by explaining that we wanted to ask some survey questions and assured them there was no "right" or "wrong" answers. They agreed and we started, but with the intention to ask how they knew if their answers were true.

Where did the stars and moon and sun come from?
Did someone create them?
When were they created?
Why do some plants have good fruit and some have bad fruit?
How do you know your answers are true?
Is there a creator?
Where did he come from?
Is he good or bad?
Is he male or female?
Does he have children?
What language does he speak?
Does he know what you are thinking?
Are there spiritual powers in the world?
Do they have a leader?
Are they good or bad?
Are they stronger than the creator?
How do you know your answers are true?
Who were the first human beings?
Are some people bad and some good?
What will happen if people are bad?
Why do people get sick?
Why do people die?
What happens to a person when he dies?
Where does he go?
What determines where he goes?
How do you know your answers are true?
Are you afraid to die?
Where will you go when you die?
Is there a place of punishment after death?
Is there a heaven?
Who decides if a person goes to heaven or not?
How do you know your answers are true?

The answers the Aetas provided were eye opening and they didn't feel in any way that we were being disrespectful or challenging them. In fact, we had a lot of fun and most of them laughed as we worked through our list. They had answers to most of the questions or struggled to come up with something to say, but every one stumbled when we asked how they knew if their answers were true. And, finally, when we asked if they wanted to learn the truth they all gave an emphatic "Yes," and that's the response we were looking for because they'd just given us permission to tell them about God.

———————————

Our work amongst the Aetas was about to veer down a somewhat different path, which had emerged unexpectedly and became inextricably linked with our ability to effectively reach the village. As it turned out, it would be the Aeta children who would serve as the catalyst to bring many of their parents to Christ—and it happened after they "invaded" America.

10.

We Took a Village

I was reading through a Newsweek magazine while getting my hair cut one day, and as I flipped through the pages I saw something that would lead Krys and I on one of the greatest adventures of our lives. Inside was a colorful two-page spread inviting people to enter a worldwide contest sponsored by KLM Airlines. KLM was celebrating its 75th Anniversary, claiming to be the world's oldest passenger airline. In commemoration of the event KLM created an international contest called *Bridging the World*, which invited people to propose ideas demonstrating how an international bridging endeavor—bringing cultures together—could be realized.

I stopped by a newsstand on the way home and bought my own copy of the magazine to show Krys then proceeded to tell her I was going to enter the contest. The prize winners would receive 25 free airplane tickets to fly round-trip anywhere that KLM flew, including routes covered by Northwest Airlines which was its affiliated US-based sister airline. Additional expenses would be taken care of for the First Prize winners such as hotels, meals and ground transportation. Second Prize winners would also receive the 25 free tickets, but any additional expenses wouldn't be covered.

My initial idea was simple—fly American Sunday school children from our home church in the states to the Philippines where they could visit the Aeta children in their village. But I wasn't convinced it was worthy of consideration, so I came up with another idea. I felt compelled to attempt something crazy that would get the attention of KLM, so I submitted a letter proposing that we fly Aeta children to America where they could visit Sunday school children in our home church.

KLM's terms and conditions stated they reserved the right to allow media teams to follow the Grand Prize winner and use photos and video footage at

75

their discretion, in order to promote their company. I understood their right to seek publicity, but I felt that such exposure of the Aeta children would be counter-productive to our work in the village and perhaps create unnecessary problems in the future—such as tourists wanting to visit tribal children they read about in an in-flight magazine. I took it to the Lord and prayed that we wouldn't be the Grand Prize winner, if in fact our proposal was named as one of the winners. I don't know if many people specifically pray about not winning a grand prize, but I did.

About two months later, Krys pulled an envelope embossed with KLMs logo out of our mailbox, which she brought home and we opened it together. The letter said they received more than 12,000 entries from around the world, and after careful review our proposal was chosen as one of the second-place winners. I was speechless. Many years prior to that, while living in Tulsa, I entered a drawing and won a new VHS video tape recorder when I signed an apartment rental contract in a new complex. I didn't own a TV at the time and ended up giving it to a co-worker who was struggling as a single mother. Winning that VCR paled in comparison to winning a worldwide contest!

* * *

I was overwhelmed with excitement as I read the letter from KLM. We were advised to contact the Northwest Airlines business office in downtown Manila for more information. Sadly, my excitement soon changed to irritation while meeting with the designated airline representative. Apparently, KLM's corporate office in Amsterdam chose the winners and instructed the various international branch offices to work with the respective winners in their geographical locations. In our case, Northwest Airlines was KLM's affiliate partner serving the Manila to U.S. routes, and the Filipino Northwest liaison wasn't very supportive of KLM's decision. She was absolutely convinced the U.S. Embassy would not issue travel visas for undocumented tribal kids, and she tried her best to coerce me to forfeit the prize and let an alternate take our place. Furthermore, she was somewhat emphatic in telling me the Philippine Government would never issue passports to the kids because they didn't have birth certificates, so there was no point even trying. I swallowed my growing frustration with the woman and decided to take her objection as a challenge. I told her that we would give it a try and take it step by step—promising to notify her immediately if we ran into any challenges that prohibited us from getting the legal documents we needed.

After my meeting at Northwest's office, we invited Pastor Joey and Beth to come to Manila because we had some exciting news to share. After a long bus ride from Bataan they anxiously sat down on the rattan furniture (*sala* set) in our living room and listened intently as I shared the entire story—the contest, my proposal and winning the plane tickets. I then asked if they would be willing to join us as chaperones.

Needless to say, they were beside themselves with the news that we had won this contest and then to hear that we were inviting them to participate in an amazing adventure. After their initial excitement settled Beth shared a personal story with us. She confided that God had previously impressed on her heart that she would be going to the U.S., although she didn't know why or how because they certainly didn't have anyone to sponsor their visa, much less have enough money to pay for tickets. However, as an act of faith, she created a handmade symbolic plane ticket and placed it inside her bible where she kept it hidden—never showing it to anyone. I think that fake ticket created an added incentive for her to effectively manage the challenges we were about to face.

I confided to Joey and Beth what the Northwest representative had told me. I also admitted our personal limitations; explaining that Krys and I didn't have the ability as foreigners to work with the Philippine Government, specifically the Department of Foreign Affairs, in order to apply for the legal documentation required for passport processing. I detailed additional logistical concerns I had, but suggested that we pray and ask God for favor with a commitment to walk it out one step at a time.

* * *

Clearly, the first step was to discuss the news with the village elders and ask if they felt comfortable with us taking a group of their children to America—although they had no idea where America was or how long it would take to walk there. Surprisingly, getting their permission wasn't difficult at all. The elders were in agreement. There was, however, one non-negotiable they insisted we honor. The chief and one of the respected village women would accompany the children. We fully agreed and felt their request was actually very prudent.

Once we gained their blessings, the elders recommended which children would be the best candidates for the trip. However, the next step shed some light on just how difficult this was going to be. Beth advised that we needed to create birthdays for each Aeta because none of them had birth certificates. In fact, they didn't even know their date of birth!

Beth knew exactly what to do. Several days later she went into the village and placed a chair under the shade of the large mango tree and individually called the selected children to stand in front of her. She asked each one how old they were and told them to state their birthday. Neither the children nor their parents had answers, which elicited a lot of laughter. Beth carefully looked over each child as if she was inspecting him or her and estimated how old she thought the child might be. Then she picked a birth-date that popped into her head. For example, she would say something like this; "You look like you might be 15 or 16 years old so I'll choose 16, and I think you were born on June 15." That information, along with their full name was typed onto a birth certificate form and submitted to the provincial Civil Registrar's Office for processing. We had certified government-issued birth certificates in our hands within a week. I couldn't believe it!

The next step was to make a formal request from the Philippine Government that passports be issued for each of those children (and the two Aeta adults) who were now legally recognized by the government. Beth met us in Manila and we accompanied her to the Department of Foreign Affairs, which had a first-come-first-served policy. Approximately 10 million Filipinos live and work overseas on temporary work visas in order to help provide financially for their families, and an additional one million people apply each year through various employment agencies. Each applicant obviously requires a passport to secure the necessary work visa before they can depart the country.

The U.S. Embassy in Manila is the second busiest American embassy in the world. The line to get inside used to be so long that Filipinos paid people to stand in line for them—sometimes all night—as they tried to apply for a visa to enter the States. When I first saw the crowd of people outside the Department of Foreign Affairs building I thought it would take all day just to get inside the building and we didn't have anyone to stand in line for us, but Beth was determined. Beth felt that our situation warranted some justified determination, so she cut in line. I followed as she made her way toward the front to speak with a security guard. Apparently, she thought it was pointless to stand in line because she believed we would be referred to an office separate from the counters where everyone one else was being processed. Sure enough. After explaining our situation to the guard, he led us to someone in a separate office who seemed to be a mid-level officer. Beth was very transparent and explained our work amongst the Aetas and winning the contest. The gentleman listened intently then took us to the top floor where we were introduced to the Secretary of Foreign Affairs who was the Philippine Government's equivalent to the U.S. Secretary of State.

The bible speaks about spiritual gifts, and each of us are encouraged to walk in them. Favor isn't named as one of those gifts, but it very well could be because I've watched in awe as some people, such as Beth, have an ability to utterly disarm government officials due to what I consider to be nothing less than God's favor on them. I was in awe as Beth respectfully, yet persuasively told our story to the Secretary as he listened intently. She described how she made up birth dates, then got the birth certificates printed and registered, which she had neatly organized in the folder sitting in her lap. She continued without pause and explained we were there to request Philippine passports be issued for each child so that we may apply for the appropriate visitor visas from the U.S. Embassy located just down the road along the shores of Manila Bay. The Secretary was understandably very professional in his mannerisms, but I noticed he was quite enthralled with Beth's narrative. Her presentation had been so thorough the Secretary didn't really have any questions, nor did he need additional clarity. He then turned to his assistant who had been standing politely to the side of his desk and instructed him to accommodate our request and prepare a new passport for each Aeta. Again, I couldn't believe what just occurred and Beth just smiled at me.

* * *

I assumed the U.S. Embassy would automatically grant the visitor visas, considering we had Philippine passports for each Aeta. We provided a copy of the Newsweek magazine detailing the contest, the letter I had written to KLM and their formal letter stating I had won as printed on their corporate letterhead. Surprisingly, the U.S. consular official had no hesitation issuing the visas to the Aetas, but he did have problem with the others we'd invited to accompany us. Sixteen Aeta children had been chosen to go on the trip plus the chief and one of the adult women — 18 Aetas in total. We felt it was important to have additional people join us so we chose three more adults in addition to Joey and Beth for a total of five Filipino chaperones. Inclusive of Krys and I, this brought the total count to 25 people which is the number of tickets KLM awarded.

The U.S. consular official, who was sitting behind three-inch-thick bulletproof security glass, told us that he had a problem with the other five, which really took me by surprise. Surely any objection would have been limited to the Aetas I'd assumed, but just the opposite happened. The official said the Aetas provided no security risk, but the other five did. He explained that the five chaperones lacked a compelling reason and evidence to return to the Philippines, which is generally based on proof of land or home ownership, sizable bank accounts, employment contracts, and substantial income that tied them to their home country. The security risk the official was referring to is known as "flight risk" and the Aetas had no reason to flee once they hit the United States.

TNT (*Tago ng Tago*) means always hiding — a Filipino expression referring to people who legally visit America, but never return to their home country. They're subsequently classified as illegal immigrants and "always hide" from U.S. Immigration officials. Unfortunately, this adversely affects other Filipinos wishing to visit the U.S. and have every intention of returning home. Due to the huge number of TNTs the embassy requires all visa applicants to prove their intention to return other than simply saying so.

An argument often used by applicants is to advise the embassy that their children will not travel with them, assuming that is sufficient incentive to return. However, many TNTs leave their children behind in hopes of figuring out how to immigrate them to the U.S. in the future, or they believe the separation is worth the sacrifice if they can find a job and send money back to them.

As the consular was explaining his reluctance to issue visas for the five chaperones, I silently prayed under my breath, "Lord, from the moment I submitted my proposal to KLM I've said that I don't want to be a part of this if you're not involved. I won the contest and was denied a First-Place award, which is exactly what I prayed for. Then we secured the passports which I also thought was impossible, and now we're hitting a barrier. If taking these kids to the U.S. is within your will then please give us favor with this official." The consular then paused for a long moment, then he suddenly agreed to issue the visitor visas for everyone. Again, I couldn't believe it!

* * *

What to do with the Aetas once we arrived in the U.S. was a legitimate concern that we discussed extensively. We were very sensitive to the fact these were tribal people from a remote village with a somewhat limited worldview. They weren't primitive and they had contact with outsiders, unlike like the stories Don Richardson or Bruce Olson describe in their missionary books regarding the people they targeted who were truly primitive. These Aetas were well beyond that. As aborigines, they hadn't integrated with lowland Filipinos, but they were involved to some degree as they traded in the marketplaces and received government workers in their village at various times who were conducting a census or collecting data for health statistics. They were, however, very much disadvantaged and marginalized from the predominant Filipino society as an isolated indigenous people group.

The Aetas were very simple people and we believed it was important to limit the depth of their immersion into America, and I fully intended to isolate them from the excesses of its overly materialistic culture. The few things each Aeta family owned, in addition to their makeshift huts, were two or three sets of clothes and a pair of rubber sandals, a few pots for cooking, and some working tools such as knives and machetes (*bolos*).

My concern wasn't so much how they might respond to seeing an abundance of food in a grocery store, or taking them to "stuff-packed" stores like Walmart or Toys-R-Us where the kids would see aisles of countless toys, dolls, bicycles, balls, etc. Honestly, I was worried they wouldn't be able to reconcile all of that abundance in comparison to their limited possessions and worldview. Our intention wasn't to show them how great America was. Rather, it was to let them meet the children of our church, sing a few of their traditional native songs, and be recipients of love and respect from our home church members.

* * *

We decided it was important to create an itinerary the kids would enjoy and shelter them from the excesses described above. Thankfully, we knew an American missionary with a degree in child psychology who offered to help us plan the trip, which focused on three main events; a visit to the zoo, a drive to the mountains where they could play in the snow, and letting them spend a day at a mini putt-putt golf course. It doesn't seem like much, but the contest required the trip to be completed within 7 days, which meant we only had 5 days on the ground. A day was set aside to let them recover from jet lag, and two days were scheduled to visit one of our supporting churches in central Oregon.

It was also important that we orientate them before the trip, so Joey and Beth brought the Aetas to our church in Manila a few days before the actual flight. We did our best to carefully consider things we take for granted such as using a flush toilet, toilet paper, taking a shower, putting on a seat belt, hot water faucets, and other things we knew they'd encounter, which we did our best to explain. We also took them to a place near the Manila airport where they could watch airplanes take off and land. We spent time explaining what the plane ride would be like and where they were going, but that kept falling short. They simply couldn't grasp where their village was located, as a specific geographic point, in relation to North America. They finally understood the trip in terms of distance based on a period of time—it would take a year to ride a Jeepney from their village to America!

We decided to make the zoo the highlight of their trip. We set up a TV in the church, hooked up a video player and showed them National Geographic movies about wild animals in Africa. Their fathers had trapped monkeys in the mountains near their village, but this was their first time to see videos of hippos, giraffes, rhinoceros, lions, zebras, and elephants. The elephants really intrigued them, and asked if they would be able to see one in America. I assured them that we would indeed see an elephant!

In the meantime, our home church had been preparing to receive us, but a significant logistical problem created some challenges. At the time, Northwest flights originating from an international airport didn't serve Portland and the closest they could get us was Seattle. The church reached out to Horizon Airlines—a U.S. regional airline serving the two cities—and shared our story about the tribal children coming to America after winning the KLM contest. "It never hurts to ask," as the saying goes and after humbly asking for their assistance Horizon provided 25 free round-trip tickets between Seattle and Portland!

We certainly had everyone's attention once our group arrived at the Manila airport. Laminated ID cards with emergency contact information and a highlighted notation explaining the bearer was part of a cultural exchange, and didn't speak English, were attached to lanyards and placed around the neck of each Aeta—who were cautioned never to remove the lanyard. Flight check-in was easy because Northwest personnel had been expecting us, and we sailed through Immigration once the officials saw that each person had the appropriate passports and visas. I was thrilled at how smooth everything had gone—until we realized the departure gate was on the lower level, which was one floor down.

I don't think I've ever heard as much laughter as I did that day watching tribal kids attempt to get on an escalator! We had briefed them about toilet paper, knives and forks, hot water, and showed them movies about elephants, but it had never occurred to us that we would need to ride an escalator. They simply could not figure out how to synchronize stepping onto a moving stair while grabbing a handrail moving in unison with the stairs. They finally figured it out by doing what kids do—they just jumped on and grabbed the rail, then we watched them pile up at the bottom because they didn't know how to step off. Thankfully no one got hurt.

* * *

The entire trip went as we'd hoped. The Aetas met American children in our home church, sang their tribal songs, played in the snow and loved putt-putt golfing. We were also able to visit a trout farm at the base of Mt. Hood where they caught fish using poles and tackle. The highlight was the zoo, and their expressions were priceless when we finally got to the elephant pens. Witnessing a new adventure unfold for those kids shed light on what we take for granted, compared to people who experienced something for the first and perhaps only time in their entire life.

Our home church demonstrated incredible hospitality in making sure that our group was well taken care of. They housed us in the community center and a small army of people volunteered to help us with various logistics such as preparing meals and driving the bus. They also collected children's books, stuffed animals, various supplies for the school, and used clothing—all of which filled 50 large U-Haul moving boxes we were able to take back as checked luggage.

I kept asking the children if they were enjoying themselves (*masaya ba kayo?*) and I always received a positive response with bright smiles, but they did admit towards the end of the week that they missed their families. Everything had gone so well and we were relieved that no one got sick or lost, but I'll admit that we were exhausted when it was time to head back to the Philippines. Only one unfortunate event occurred which, thankfully, had been limited to involving the older Aeta woman. Everyone was fast asleep during the long flight back across the Pacific Ocean when the main feature movie was shown on the drop down TV screen. I hadn't noticed the movie starting and was shocked when I looked up to see Stephen Spielberg's hit movie *Jurassic Park* was playing. I immediately thought to myself that she doesn't realize the dinosaurs are CGI-animation and she's going to think they're real. The Aeta woman was wide awake, sitting in a chair diagonally across from where I was sitting. Overwhelmed with terror she finally hid under her blanket when the T-Rex ate the guy sitting in the outhouse. We tried to explain to her later that it was all pretend, but she didn't seem to believe us because the movie made them appear so lifelike.

* * *

The village welcomed their children back home and it was a wonderful reunion, especially when they saw the 50 boxes full of gifts from America. Krys and I returned to our house in Manila after saying goodbye and spent several days recovering from exhaustion. A few weeks later we boarded another Northwest flight and returned to the U.S. to begin a furlough that was to be the catalyst for a new direction in our missionary life.

Krys and I didn't fully grasp the implications of that trip with the Aetas, and we were excited and honored to participate in such an amazing adventure. A few months into our furlough we started receiving updates from Joey and Beth, who shared that the trip had served as an incentive for the Aetas regarding two important things; self-preservation and a deeper response to the gospel message. Apparently, as best as Beth could explain it, the Aeta chief and the adult woman saw something in the American culture which caused them to consider the value and need for self-preservation as a village. They were able to somehow translate what they observed in America and applied it directly to their village. They had determined they couldn't protect their long-term interests without legal rights to property, so they embolden themselves to petition the Philippine Government to issue them land titles for the housing lots in their village. Two other things happened that thrilled us; several of the adults decided they needed to learn how to read and write, and started attending the school with their children. And, finally, many of the Aetas in the village embraced Christ and were water baptized.

It was a special honor when our pastor invited Pastor Joey to preach at our home church in Portland during that trip and listen to him encourage an American audience—as an imported voice from a developing country—carrying a message he believed was from the Lord of every nation, tribe and tongue.

Over these past two plus decades I've continually seen God use a multitude of things, many of which can't be explained, such as winning a worldwide contest in order to position people to hear the gospel and effect various positive transformations where people live their lives.

As we were about to discover, He was setting the stage to position us for something new.

11.

In the Margins

Our planned furlough was intentional, with the single purpose of pursuing U.S. licensing for Krys to become a Certified Professional Midwife (CPM). The previous year she applied and was accepted for enrollment at a small midwifery school based in El Paso, Texas. It was a nine-month direct-entry program using an accredited curriculum offering an Associate of Science Degree in Midwifery (ASM), which prepared students to take state and national board exams for licensing certification upon graduating.

It was a Christian-based school affiliated with a local church which had integrated the midwifery school into their lay member training and ministry outreach program. Classroom sessions were held in a modular building that had been moved onto the church property. Practical training was limited to prenatal exams, and every Wednesday Krys and her classmates were driven across the Mexican border into Juárez where pregnant women came to a building owned by YWAM for a free check-up.

The school was a full-time commitment for Krys, who stayed very busy attending classes, studying for exams, preparing group projects with her classmates, and participating in the weekly outreaches in Juárez. I did my best to stay relatively busy, and I read several books on cross-cultural missions and listened to cassette tapes on Christian leadership from the church library. I also led a home bible study under the direction of the associate pastor, Ed Johnson, and I usually drove the van that shuttled students over to Juárez.

I spent a lot of time mentally and prayerfully processing the three years we'd just spent in the Philippines and found that I had more questions coming off the mission field than I had going in—primary of which was trying to understand at a deeper level what the role of a missionary is. Our home church and supporters considered our overseas ministry successful, based on the feedback we received, but I was searching for a larger context and felt inadequate in so many ways, which caused me to wonder just how successful we had been. Doing missions without a context is just living in a foreign country.

Many of the blank pages we had arrived with on the mission field began to fill up with jumbled bits and pieces and scribblings, and those pages were being framed by recounting the things we'd experienced with the church plant in Manila and our work with Pastor Joey and the Aetas. In addition, the narrative describing our immersion into a foreign culture with new sights and sounds, and smells of the market, riding Jeepneys, eating strange food, and learning about the culture contributed a lot of filler to those pages. The margins, however, remained empty. And it was there that I wanted to jot down notes that would help shape the context I needed to understand at a deeper level where things would come together and make sense. It would be similar to writing something important in the margins of your bible when the pastor made a point about a verse you've read a hundred times, and then it finally clicks and shapes the context of a passage we've struggled to understand for so long. Suddenly everything falls into place and the margins become our own story. And, only when that happens does it become personal and helps us find our own voice which resonates within the larger story.

*　*　*

I hadn't had any formal missionary training before going to the mission field so I considered enrolling in a course to broaden my perspective in hopes it might help with the "larger context" thing with which I was struggling. I had the privilege of talking on the phone with the legendary mission strategist, Ralph Winter, founder of the U.S. Center for World Mission (USCWM), the William Carey International University, and the International Society for Frontier Missiology based in Pasadena. He had compiled and edited the *Perspectives on the World Christian Movement Reader*, which was the go-to manual on biblical, historical, cultural and strategic perspectives for global missions. Mr. Winter recommended I enroll in their Intercultural Studies program via long-distance education which I seriously considered, but the more I thought about it, I sensed it wasn't for me because the focus was on sociological and anthropological studies, which involved a lot of reading. My style of learning is experiential, not passive, which I realized as a fourth grader.

Brooklyn Elementary School had two separate classrooms for each of the six represented grades, and the kids were randomly divided between two teachers, each with their own room. My teacher, Mrs. Hensley, did a good job, but there was something entirely magical and intriguing coming from the other 4th grade classroom adjacent to ours. The teacher didn't just stand in front of his students and talk to them, like all the other teachers did. Rather, he immersed his students into the subjects. If he taught about general biology he'd show them how to make improvised crawdad traps using chicken wire stretched over a simple wood frame. Then, after school or on weekends, he invited the kids on field trips down to the Powder River behind the library and show them how to catch crawdads by wading into the shallow water and setting the traps. If he taught about the pioneers traveling along the Oregon Trail he'd arrange for someone to haul an old replica covered wagon onto the school property and have the kids pretend they were pioneers by setting up a camp next to the wagon. He taught about birds native to Oregon and had dozens of taxidermy samples scattered around his classroom for the kids to view up close. During recess his students were telling us the difference between a cedar waxwing and a yellow-tipped waxwing.

I was in the wrong class.

Sadly, the school administration was not comfortable with his out-of-the-box teaching style and terminated his employment midway through the school year. A replacement teacher was brought in, forcing his students to retreat back to the classroom, thereby effectively switching off the fascination of experiencing what they were learning. School for them went back to being boring.

I learn by doing, by watching, looking at other's models, and asking questions. I guess I tend to fall along the lines of learning according to

Aristotle's definition, "...we learn by doing them." I like the quote from Earnest Yeboah; "If you define your life by what you learn only, you will never leave great footprints on earth." The footprints I've left behind may be more indicative of someone stumbling through life, but at least I'm stumbling forward to the best of my ability.

* * *

About five months into Krys' midwifery school, the pastor of the church invited a retired missionary to speak at a three-day church planting seminar for people interested in cross-cultural evangelism and discipleship. I attended and was fascinated as he walked us through several experiential-based sessions as he systematically demonstrated how to plant a new church.

The speaker was Dr. George Patterson who had personally overseen a church planting movement involving 100 new church plants in Central America. I didn't know it at the time, but Patterson held a prominent position among well-known missiologists who were looking at world evangelization from a collective perspective as they formulated global strategies that complimented the biblical mandate. A detailed overview of Patterson's church planting strategy titled "The Spontaneous Multiplication of Churches" was published in the *Perspectives Reader.*

Dr. Patterson's strategy was an expanded Theological Education by Extension (TEE) method developed by Ralph Winter in Guatemala during the 1960s. TEE was different than the traditional system of enrolling students in an urban-based residential bible college using a typical classroom setting. Mr. Winter's model extended bible school education to small rural churches in the outlying provincial areas where enrolled lay leaders completed self-study modules at home—at their own pace as time permitted.

* * *

I'll briefly explain Patterson's strategy, which I've laid out in the next few paragraphs because it helped transition me away from the limitations of a novice missionary. What I learned from him was crucial to being a successful missionary—respective of training and equipping nationals to plant churches.

Patterson believed that bible school education should be coupled with evangelism, so he modified TEE by inserting an additional 'E' and called it TEEE—Theological Education and *Evangelism* by Extension. In addition, he felt that too much emphasis was placed on theological education, which was only one aspect of pastoral training.

Patterson also redefined the end result. Rather than the goal being a theologically educated student, he envisioned a new church plant as the goal or objective of bible school education. In order to accomplish this, he included an extension chain, or what's referred to as a Paul-Timothy link (2 Timothy 2:2) into his model as a mechanism to help form new congregations. The link involved a pastor (Paul) training a student (Timothy) how to start a new church by teaching him how to share the gospel through a web of relationships, while providing practical advice and experience.

The mechanism of how TEEE worked was actually quite simple. TEEE was introduced to rural pastors who were encouraged to enroll one or two lay leaders into the program. The pastor served as a type of professor and taught his students subjects such as church history and theology at a level similar to that offered in any urban bible school, but in a much more informal setting tailored to the needs of the students.

Students were also taught how to evangelize, but it wasn't defined by having someone repeat a sinner's prayer. Rather, it was in line with Christ's mandate; "…teaching them to obey all things, as I have commanded you." The "teaching" was done as new converts were gathered together into a home bible study for the purpose of discipleship where the lay leader taught them to obey the commands of Christ such as water baptism, participation in the Lord's supper, loving their neighbor, tithing, sharing the gospel with others, etc.

The model was entirely one-on-one in its approach and each student learned as an apprentice under the supervision of the pastor who served as the school professor. It's an apprenticeship model very similar to the way Krys was trained as a lay midwife under the direction of a qualified preceptor who was physically present in order to provide supervision during labor and delivery. The preceptor demonstrated how to manage a hemorrhage, for example, then let Krys practice exactly what was demonstrated until she became proficient.

The preceptor example is how Patterson set up his TEEE strategy. In its purest form, the TEEE model enabled a senior pastor to plant a new daughter church by training his lay leader to be the lead person. In other words, the pastor planted a daughter church *through* the lay leader. Patterson was careful to emphasize that the natural byproduct of evangelism and discipleship is church planting. New believers would be formed into a new body of believers separate from the mother church, and those new converts would become the genetic code for a new church plant—serving as an incubator for on the job pastoral training.

At some point during the seminar, Patterson said that obedience provided the motivation for ministry. He explained the incentive for students to learn was the value placed on obedience to Christ's teachings, which he termed *Obedience Oriented Education*. Patterson wrote, "All bible school work assignments are done in direct obedience to Christ. The heart of the course is our love for the Lord Jesus Christ who said, 'If you love me, keep my commandments.'" The student responds voluntarily in obedient love for Christ—not the professor, or grades or a diploma.

I felt like I was an accidental apprentice, and those three days—as brief as it might seem in terms of adequate training time—was all it took to connect the dots because I already had a foreign mission framework as a point of reference. Understanding the value of obedience as the motivation for ministry was a watershed moment for me. So often it seems that far too much energy and resources are spent on getting people to do what we wanted regarding ministry efforts rather than focusing on those who willingly desire to obey Christ voluntarily. Equipping and empowering those people for ministry was the key to being fruitful as a missionary.

That brief encounter was pivotal and clarified my understanding—some of my misunderstandings rather—of a missionary's role on the field and provided answers to the questions I'd been processing. It helped resolve some things from my past experiences as a relatively new missionary where I felt so inadequate at times and lacked clarity.

The notes in my margins, gleaned by what Patterson taught, helped shape the larger context for me and rearranged it in a way that made sense, causing all the pieces to fall into place. However, a course correction was the next step in the direction God was leading us, and He was requiring me to take a step forward—into my past.

12.

A Past Revisited

I spent several weeks processing what I'd learned in Patterson's seminar. Then early one morning I felt one of those undeniable nudges from the Holy Spirit while sitting alone in our apartment reading my bible. It was the kind of prodding that solicits our participation beyond simply confessing a sin or promising to stop complaining or judging other people. God isn't one to be paraphrased, but the dialog went something like this;

God: "You need to apologize for lying to your former boss when you worked at the gas station."

Me: "But it's been 17 years."

God: " I've been asking you to deal with this for 17 years."

Me: "But..."

God: "But nothing. I'm not going to bless your ministry beyond its present level if you don't resolve this."

The extended version of that dialog went on for several days because I thought the validity of addressing something I'd done years before was not worth being brought back into the forefront. I likened my theft at that gasoline station more to youthful foolishness, like the time I stole something from my friend when I was about five years old. Years later, during the course of a conversation, I told him what I'd done and we both made light of it as simply being the things kids do.

Each time I tried to change the conversation with God, He wouldn't. I'd heard someone say the farther you go with God the less options you have. He was leading me back into an old story that needed to be resolved, but on His terms.

At various times, and over the course of many years, the Holy Spirit had been gently prompting me to contact my former boss and make restitution for the actual amount of money I'd stolen. But this time the prodding turned into a match of wills I couldn't contest, and it was no longer a subtle conviction.

"I'm not going to bless your ministry beyond its present level" wasn't a reprimand as if I was getting a lecture. Instead, it came as an encouraging word of affirmation as if God was saying, "Look, it's the right thing to do and we're going to do this together. But I'm not going to let this go until you do it." I've had enough experiences with the Lord to know that I tend to rise taller after kneeling down in response to the Holy Spirit, so I surrendered and agreed it was worth the risk.

I was so ashamed of what I'd done to my boss at the time and the embarrassment I brought to my dad that I struggled to do whatever it took to walk away from that scene played out 17 years ago, maintaining some sense of self-worth. So, I lied to protect my pride. I'd actually stolen more than I admitted and that conviction stayed with me for years, although I'd done my best to try and bury it.

Krys smiled when I filled her in on the storyline. I suggested it would be a waste of time because my former boss had probably moved on to another town and it would be impossible to track him down. To prove my assumption, I dialed the phone number for information and got an operator. I identified the state and city and the name of my previous boss, then I heard a robotic voice state the phone number for the person I was looking for. It turned out that he hadn't moved from my hometown and still lived in the same house. I think the blood drained from my face as I sat down next to Krys and showed her the phone number. She looked at me and said, "Bummer!"

I could have written him a letter and enclosed a check, but I knew it needed to be more personal. Besides, God had made it very clear regarding what He would and would not accept to make this right before He would bless my ministry. It took a few days to build up enough courage to call my former boss, and I finally dialed the number. When someone answered, I asked to speak with Don. "May I tell him who's calling please?" I replied that I'd rather surprise him. As I sensed the phone being handed to Don, my heart rate picked up. I asked Don if he remembered me to which he said

"Yes." I then asked if he remembered my theft. He said that he remembered. I asked if he remembered the episode involving my dad paying him the money I'd stolen, and he also replied with a "Yes."

I then stepped into a narrative I'd been rehearsing in my mind over and over again.

"I realize this sounds ridiculous, but I've been meaning to call you for 17 years because I stole more money from you than what I admitted. I'm serving in ministry as a foreign missionary and God has been dealing with me to resolve this issue. I'm embarrassed to call and admit this after so many years, but I want to apologize for what I did and I need to repay you the true amount that I stole."

There was a short pause, then Don said it wasn't necessary and suggested I just keep the money in the ministry. I replied and said, "I guessed you might say something like that, but God instructed me that I am not to accept your offer. It's personally important that I send you the money, but there's a small problem. Honestly, and I mean honestly, I really can't remember how much I stole from you because it happened so long ago. So, if it's OK with you I'm going to take a good guess then add a little extra just to make sure." He said that was OK and gave me the address to send my check.

Before the call ended I asked why he hadn't press charges against me when all the evidence proved I'd committed a crime. Don said he knew I was a good kid and it was just a stupid mistake I'd made. Then I asked if anyone else had ever called him to admit they had stolen money and wanted to apologize. Don said there had indeed been one other person who called him a few years ago, and recounted a similar story about stealing from his business. He said he was also a missionary serving somewhere in South America.

Krys gave me one of those, I'm proud to be your wife looks after I hung up the phone. The next day, during my quiet time alone with the Lord, I recalled for Him my good deed and expected to receive a *job well done* word of affirmation. Instead, the impression I got was more like Him whispering, "You shouldn't have stolen the money in the first place."

I discovered something in that storyline I was pulled back into. There is value in learning to follow Jesus with a limp.

That experience along with having an enhanced grasp of cross-cultural mission strategy helped me feel empowered to return to the field with a new understanding of my role as a missionary. Or at least I thought I did.

I was about to step into a mission experience, as described in the chapters that follow, where I unknowingly set up a dependence on myself, although with good intentions, because I thought my role or expectation was to serve as the lead character, based on the fact that I had a strategy. However, the success of my missionary career would eventually lead to a conversion experience at its very height. What I didn't realize at the time is that I wasn't converted at a place I needed to be—and from that place my role was redefined.

Shortly after I mailed a check to my former boss, Krys and I were thrown an unexpected curve ball. We were about to be redirected to a new location and fully immersed into a community of crushing poverty where we would direct an international team serving thousands of people living in a place where corruption was systemic, oppression was commonplace, and abysmal inequality made life incredibly difficult for people in our future target group.

Running parallel to that community-based outreach would be the emergence of a secondary ministry that would, quite unexpectedly, be embraced and funded by the third wealthiest family in the Philippines whose influence offered an unprecedented opportunity to see youth deeply impacted by the gospel message using an innovative program no one else had tried.

I lacked a category in which to put the experience we were about to undertake. God was leading Krys and I to a place that all other missionaries we knew in the Philippines, including the U.S. Government, warned Americans to avoid.

13.

Village of Death

It's been my experience that once a perception of risk is introduced into the equation of life, God eases us into difficult decisions while walking it out with us at a manageable pace and provides enough assurances to help us step into our fear. Krys and I were a few months from completing our furlough with the intention of returning to Manila and continuing our missionary work when God began to stir our hearts concerning a major transition. It was entirely unexpected and caused us some uncomfortable apprehension.

An idea had been presented to me by Ed Johnson, the associate pastor of the church we were attending in El Paso where the midwifery school was located. Ed was about 15 years my senior and befriended me shortly after arriving. He expressed a genuine interest in our missionary work, and he shared many of his own personal stories and wisdom he'd gleaned from his life experiences while serving in ministry for many years.

I believe some of the best ministry happens through a relationship, which places us in a position to speak into the lives of people we care about and want to see them move in the right direction. Krys and I were about six months into our time in El Paso when Ed wondered if God was trying to get my attention. As I've gotten older, I've observed at times that mature Christians are able to discern God working in the background at a level other people sometimes miss.

One day, while having lunch together at a local Mexican restaurant, Ed asked if I would consider praying about relocating to Mindanao — the large southern island of the Philippines located about 600 miles south of Manila. The idea was prompted because the church had started an informal School of Missions the year before we arrived in El Paso. A young lady by the name of

Ramona, who had graduated from the midwifery school the year prior to Krys' enrollment had just moved to Davao City which is a commercial port city in the southern central coast of Mindanao. She had moved there in order to start a charity birthing clinic with a proposed vision to provide maternal healthcare for poor women while also serving as a site for American midwives to volunteer after completing their midwifery academic studies in El Paso.

Ed suggested Krys and I might want to prayerfully consider joining that new work. He had been a successful businessman in his earlier years and I think his advice was based on two perspectives. From a very practical standpoint, he recognized the need for a single woman to have people come alongside her, particularly a married couple because a team had not accompanied her to start the new work. In retrospect that decision should have been considered more carefully due to the burdens Ramona was shouldering alone. Ed also knew that Dr. Patterson's teaching had a profound impact on me and he recognized the opportunity to see an expanded ministry develop as an outreach of the clinic. Ed suggested I consider overseeing a church planting effort to work in harmony with the clinic where Krys could help deliver babies and serve as a preceptor for aspiring midwives needing clinical experience.

It was incredibly difficult for Krys and I to even consider Ed's proposal. It seems, however, that God, in His patience and understanding of our frailties, allows us the time we need to process certain decisions, especially when they come along unexpectedly. The thought of relocating meant we'd have to redirect away from the ministries where we'd served in Manila and Bataan, and in effect let go of the partnerships we'd developed with the nationals and other missionaries. We didn't take this decision lightly and spent weeks praying about it. Initially, attempting to get clarity was a bit muddled, but once we laid down our apprehension we began to see more clearly that the Lord was in fact asking us to change direction and look south, so we finally surrendered and said "Yes."

As our nine-month furlough was winding down we spent time visiting our supporting churches and advising people regarding our planned transition to Mindanao. Then, on August 8, 1996, we boarded a plane for

Davao City, the country's third largest city, with a population, at that time, of about one million people.

* * *

The southern Philippine island of Mindanao is considered to be one of the most volatile places in all of Southeast Asia—shaken by unrelenting internal strife and war. Four separate rebel factions; the MILF (Moro Islamic Liberation Front), MNLF (Moro National Liberation Front), the Abu Sayyaf, and the communist NPA (New People's Army) have been at war with the national government for decades. Thousands of innocent people have been killed or wounded as a direct result of these various factions vying for power and independence from the centralized government based in Manila.

Most experts believe the root cause of the unrest stem from disputes over rightful land ownership, and the Muslims who occupy much of the western provinces feeling disenfranchised and unrepresented by the so-called Imperialistic wealthy political classes based in Manila—all of which is fueled by millions of people enduring the challenges of grinding poverty; and Mindanao has the country's most impoverished provinces. The activities of these rebels and their inclinations towards violence and random acts of terrorism are exacerbated by their access to illegal firearms, which greatly hinders the national government's ability to enforce laws in the vast provincial areas.

The problem has become so widespread that the national police force is unable to deal with all the strife and conflicts, resulting in the Philippine Army battling with the rebels at various times that ebb and flow with the political climate and the gravity of the atrocities perpetuated by the rebels. As a result, regional economies suffer because large companies are fearful of investing in infrastructure and new businesses that would employ people.

Criminal activities and kidnapping by these factions became such a problem that the U.S. State Department issued travel warnings through its Embassy in Manila, advising Americans to stay away from Mindanao, especially the southwestern regions due to the heightened risks against Americans. This was the primary reasons Krys and I were so apprehensive about moving to Mindanao. In 1991, two American evangelists were killed when the Abu Sayyaf launched a grenade attack in Zamboanga City and later bombed the MV Doulos, a Christian missionary ship, killing six and injuring 32 while it was docked in Zamboanga. In 1993, they bombed a cathedral in Davao City, killing six people and kidnapping another American missionary working on a translation project later that same year. Any time the word "Mindanao" was mentioned among missionaries while living in Manila, it was usually followed with the exhortation, "Stay away from there!"

* * *

Ramona had set up the new clinic in the heart of Agdao, an impoverished area with 100,000 people living in 13 barrios (*barangays*), which stretched 1 kilometer along the bay and inland about 1 kilometer—100,000 people packed into 1 square kilometer. Multiple squatter communities were scattered throughout much of Agdao and the clinic was situated at the crossroads of two adjoining barangays full of squatters.

A squatter community is an area of any size, whether a single lot or several city blocks inhabited by poor families lacking the financial ability to buy land. Generally, the people living in these communities are a combination of urban poor born in the city and those who migrated from the provincial areas looking for jobs. They "squat" by occupying and building makeshift houses on any available lot or piece of land not fenced or guarded by an on-site tenant. Any vacant piece of land, no matter how small, is an opportunity to occupy. Squatter houses are stacked or built on top of one another once the actual land area is used up in order to make space for more people. I've seen families living in makeshift shacks stacked five high where dozens, if not hundreds of families may take up illegal residence in a relatively small area.

Squatting becomes a complex problem for city officials. The local economy needs laborers, drivers, cooks, maids, etc. but there's a shortage of housing to accommodate the influx of people coming in from the surrounding regions to fill these jobs. It's been estimated that 25% of the 20 million people living in Manila are squatters and once people squat on the land it's very difficult to get them off. Although they have no formal rights, the law states that a land owner cannot legally evict squatters without a court order, which takes years to secure. Even with such an order in hand the owner is sometimes obligated to find a new lot for them to relocate to, fund the cost to rent trucks to move their belongings, and pay each family a handsome sum for all the inconvenience. And this only happens after the squatters have organized themselves and engage the landowner on their terms where they are assured their best interests will be accommodated. The landowner always gets the short end of the deal—even though it's his land to which he legally holds the title.

* * *

The few foreigners living in Davao at that time rented houses in areas of the city located far away from Agdao. Krys and I, however, felt that we needed to live in Agdao since our missionary work would be based there. While living in Manila I heard about a mission organization that mobilized Western missionaries to be fully immersed in squatter communities and live in improvised makeshift houses in order to take on a similar lifestyle—sort of like becoming incarnate with the people so they could better identify with them.

Personally, I didn't feel it was necessary to live at that level for a couple of reasons. First, I'd heard squatters comment that although they respected the missionaries willing to live in their communities and understood their motives, they also knew that a missionary could easily extract himself from the situation to get the care they needed, such as medical care in the private hospitals, or if they needed a break they could go on furlough and return to a Western lifestyle. The squatters didn't have those options, so in a sense they felt, to a small extent, that missionaries attempting to live like them were somewhat hypocritical. Secondly, the statistics for missionary burnout is highest amongst those who live among the poor.

Thankfully, we were able to rent a small two-story duplex with a concrete floor located about 200 meters from the newly opened clinic. It was about twenty years old and infested with termites, and rats were often seen scurrying between the walls separating our duplex from the one next door. A six-foot high fence separated us from several squatters who lived on one side of the apartment and a taxi barn on the other side where mechanics kept dilapidated taxis running and drivers were coming and going 24/7. Drunks wailing their favorite songs with karaoke music blaring late into the night—at almost unbearable decibel levels—made it difficult to sleep. Roosters, which men raised for cock fighting, crowed all hours of the day and dogs constantly barking only added to the noise. Every morning the neighbor at the back of our house started a wood fire to cook his food and thick smoke would fill our house. Neighbors on the other side burned their garbage every day, carrying toxic smells of burning plastic into our apartment.

We didn't live like the locals but we were very much their neighbors, separated only by that fence. We witnessed how they lived and the tremendous difficulties they faced as a result of the injustices of poverty they endured and how it affected them. Living in the conditions into which the poor are immersed is incredibly raw and so different than anything I'd experienced growing up in a middle-class family. We didn't see the injustices laid upon the shoulders of our neighbors firsthand. Rather we saw the effect of injustice people were immersed into, often without any relief.

I had read about urban violence, but I had no idea concerning the magnitude of urban war that had been waged in the neighborhood prior to our arrival—until people started telling me their stories. The locals referred to Agdao as the *Village of Death* (*Barrio Patay*), which was "stained in blood" as one newspaper described it. In the 1980s communist rebels, specifically the NPA, had a strong presence in Agdao, which at that time was basically an urban shantytown. Agdao became known as *Nicaragdao* because people associated it with the Nicaraguan Revolution where the Sandinistas engaged in a systematic campaign of terror and intimidation amongst the general public. The NPA demanded money or stole from the people, justifying it as revolutionary taxes, and they used intimidation and killing to get attention for their politically motivated causes. On the other hand, some of the government military forces fighting the NPA were also extorting money from the very same people they were supposed to be helping. The general population was caught in the middle, and the ongoing cycle of violence between the government and the rebels had polarized the population. Violence was at its worst in Agdao and it became known as the murder capital of the entire country. It eventually escalated to the point that innocent people starting getting killed, and almost every day two or three bodies were found lying in the streets. Everyone stayed away from Agdao unless they were one of the unfortunate thousands who to lived there as a result of circumstances beyond their control.

After many years, right-wing counterinsurgency groups rose up such as Alsa Masa (*masses arise*), which had been equipped by the military to serve as hit squads known as "sparrow units" to go after the NPA's hit squads who were assassinating police and soldiers. Alsa Masa finally succeeded in driving the rebels from the Agdao area and effectively took control, but the long-term violence had left a polarizing effect on the community.

I don't think I've ever been to a place where people seemed so disengaged with one another. We found deep-rooted negative psychological residual evidence amongst most people and discovered that no one trusted anyone. As a missionary, it's important to understand the history of the people and it took a while to figure out the reason for such distrust. I remember a conversation with a man who said it was impossible to be neutral during those years of so much violence, and there were always consequences. For example, if the people turned to the government for help the rebels claimed the people were siding with the government they were trying to overthrow; and the same accusations came from the government if the people sided with the rebels. Although the people were friendly towards us they were unusually timid and kept to themselves.

* * *

Ramona had done an excellent job getting the clinic up and running. She was able to glean advice from other Christian organizations and secured the assistance of a Christian attorney who helped her register the clinic as a legal entity, as required by Philippine law. In addition, and much to her credit, Ramona went to great lengths to build relationships with the local government officials and explain why she was setting up a charity-based healthcare center. The time she invested in those relationships effectively dissolved any apprehension or distrust people may have had concerning the idea of foreigners starting a new clinic in Agdao.

Furthermore, Ramona built alliances with the local traditional birth attendants (*hilots*) who generally don't have any formal education or training. Most of their knowledge is acquired through indigenous methods and passing down of skills from previous generations. A Hilot (short for *manghihilot*) draws from a variety of means to help her patients, which may include her folk knowledge of herbs, animism beliefs, amulets, etc. A common postpartum practice hilots use, especially in the remote rural areas, is something called *Suob* which involves whole body massages on the mother after the baby is born. They advise the patient not to bathe for several days, and on a prescribed day a mixture of herbs is burned in a large skillet and the patient straddles it with a loose-fitting towel or blanket wrapped around her that catches the smoke in her lower areas. The practice is supposed to drive away any negative influences brought on by the birthing experiences. I'll fast forward briefly to share a quick story about Krys who was managing a lengthy labor at the clinic when her patient wasn't progressing very well. She stepped out of the delivery room for a few moments and discovered her patient had disappeared when she walked back into the room. The patient's husband pointed outside where Krys found the patient's mother waving smoke up her daughter's dress while she was straddled over a pile of burning grass. The patient eventually delivered, but Krys wasn't too keen on giving credit to the grandmother's attempt at smoking the baby out of the womb!

Ramona looked beyond any animistic or folk practices of the hilots and built bridges by seeking their advice regarding their style of labor and delivery practices. Her soft-spoken, introverted and shy mannerism worked tremendously in her favor because people found Ramona to be gentle and kindhearted, unlike most foreigners who tend to be louder than typical Filipinos and a little too frank and candid than what their culture is accustomed to.

Davao was obviously new to us, but we hadn't arrived there with the same sense of idealism and naiveté we had when we first stepped off the plane in Manila as new missionaries almost four years prior. We had learned a lot during those formative years and had a fair share of experience on which to draw. We felt relatively well prepared to begin a new work, but we soon found ourselves faced with an unexpected problem.

Soon after getting settled into our apartment Ramona privately confided to us concerning the amount of stress she was feeling. During the previous 12 months, she had invested a considerable amount of time and energy to establish an entirely new work—without the help and support of a team. About two months before our arrival a handful of short-term missionaries from America and Canada arrived in Davao to work in the clinic as midwife apprentices. Hosting them in addition to training her national midwife staff, while also managing a growing support staff, was a full-time job for Ramona. The fact that she lived upstairs in the clinic with the short-term missionaries and the Filipino midwives only added to her stress because people were calling on her all hours of the day and night. It was readily evident that it was all taking a toll on her.

Ramona would oftentimes walk down to our apartment during the early evening hours and share with us how difficult the job was becoming and freely admitted that her gifting wasn't administrative. We did our best to encourage and assure her that we were there to help by any means necessary, which we did. Much to our surprise, several weeks later Ramona confided that she was considering stepping away from her role as the director. Four months later she resigned and left the country. No one else was in a position to step into leadership so the clinic was turned over to us, which is not what we envisioned nor expected would happen when we decided to relocate to Davao.

* * *

In the book *Outliers*, Malcolm Gladwell introduced what he termed the "10,000-Hour Rule," which according to him is the time it takes to become proficient at a sport or musical instrument. People claim that rule also applies to management because, as they suggest, it takes that long to become proficient in their roles regarding a comprehensive understanding of their job. It actually works out to about five years if you compute it based on a typical 40-hour work week. Krys and I didn't have five hours of direct management experience related to the clinic when we took over, and we soon found ourselves on an accelerated learning curve.

We did our best to grow in our role as the new directors, and it was incredibly challenging at times. Neither of us had sufficient administrative experience needed to manage a medical clinic while overseeing different nationalities with diverse values and communication styles.

By the end of our first year the cross-cultural team had swelled to 30 people, which included a Filipino national staff numbering seven full-time midwives and six support staff. The patient load had increased considerably and we started hiring additional staff to help accommodate the growth in the number of births. A total of 573 babies had been delivered during our first 12 months and we anticipated the numbers to increase exponentially simply because the services were offered free of charge. In addition, we were hosting several foreign short-term midwife apprentices who were volunteering under the direct supervision and oversight of licensed Filipino midwives we had employed.

It was during this first year that an opportunity was presented for us to provide foster care for an eight-month old Filipino baby girl named Josephine or "Josie" for short. After several months we decided to adopt her, but there was a slight problem. The social worker advised us that Philippine law didn't allow foreigners to adopt domestically from within the country. We continued to provide a home for Josie and prayed the legislature would change the laws. Then after three long years, we received news that the Philippine Government passed Republic Act 8552 otherwise known as the Domestic Adoption Act. We fulfilled the requirements stipulated by the new law, and after a court hearing the judge signed the adoption decree which directed the Civil Registrar's Office to amend Josie's birth certificate showing Krys and me as her legal parents. The social worker told us that our case as foreigners seeking to adopt a child within country was the first case to test the new law and people were watching to see how the judge would rule. I'm not so sure if that was true, but several missionaries started adopting Filipino children in the following years.

Five years later, we went through the process again when we adopted our second Filipino daughter, Jessica, who came to us when she was one year old. The tragic event of 9/11 separated Josie's and Jessica's adoptions and there was a vast difference between how the U.S. Government processed the citizenship papers for both girls. Josie, being adopted before 9/11 was issued a travel visa and granted citizenship fairly easy compared to Jessica who was adopted after 9/11. The creation of the Department of Homeland Security after 9/11 and the subsequent scrutiny people were subjected to in order to secure citizenship for a foreign child adopted by U.S. expats residing in that foreign country became incredibly arduous and very frustrating. Sadly, I'll admit that we chose not to adopt other children after Jessica because of the extraordinary challenges we would have been forced to endure, which were becoming even more stressful based on the stories we'd heard from other missionaries. Some missionary friends who also adopted a Filipino child have been waiting almost ten years to navigate through the process, and they continue to wait even as I'm writing this.

I never considered adopting children prior to having Josie come into our house as a foster child. Many people have asked what it's like to adopt foreign children and I reply with a smile that it's incomprehensible to consider loving my own biological children, if we could have had our own, any more than I love Josie and Jessica. They are the light of our lives.

* * *

The clinic didn't look anything like you might expect. In fact, it didn't look anything like a clinic at all. It was a simple two story wood framed house built on concrete slab sometime during the early 1970s. I estimated the size to be about 3,000 square feet. The ground floor had a sizable kitchen, a large open living room, and three very small bedrooms that served as labor and delivery rooms. The upstairs had been refurbished to accommodate eight small bedrooms that were barely large enough for a twin-sized bunkbed and a small side table. It appeared that the owner intended to use it as a rental property investment and had renovated it to serve as a border house where people rent a room and share a common kitchen.

The house was situated about 30 meters off the main road, fronting the entrance of a squatter community separated by a stagnant body of water about 500 square meters in size. It became the default dumping ground where many of the patients discarded their placentas. Water hyacinth floated freely on top of the water which was about two feet deep. Experts claim hyacinth negatively impacts healthy biodiversity, but over the years we observed that the high nitrogen content in the plants contained some sort of beneficial ecological bio-cleansing ability that broke down the placentas and made the water clean enough for local wildlife such as rats and frogs to procreate in abundance!

* * *

Our patients came from impoverished families, and many external factors work against those families causing them to become victims of forces that present overwhelming obstacles as they struggle to climb out of poverty. A typical squatter family lives in an area the size of an American walk-in closet they've either rented or fabricated out of coconut lumber, thin plywood and a rusted metal roof with no running water or toilet, while cooking their meals over an open fire because most cannot afford the propane tank used to fuel a small table-top burner. Two substandard wires bring in electricity tapped from an electrical meter shared by several neighbors. Every aspect of life is a daily struggle for these squatters whose families can number up to 12–14, or even higher. The wife may earn ₱2,000–3,000 per month (about $50) washing clothes while her husband drives a Jeepney, which he pays a boundary fee to rent for 12 hours. After paying the fee, fuel, his partner who collects fare money, and the occasional payoff to the traffic police, his take-home earnings are about ₱250 a day—about half the amount the government claims is the daily cost of living for impoverished families. Any amount the wife is able to save is generally wiped out each time one of the children gets sick and needs medical attention, which frequently happens due to their poor diet and unsanitary living conditions.

The clinic was situated in the middle of Agdao, offering free maternal healthcare, which squatter families previously never had access to. Every patient who came through the door was prayed for, and as a result of the long-term relational aspect, it provided the midwives with immense favor, unprecedented insight and access into the lives of these impoverished families. A patient developed a natural trust with their midwife who would listen to their stories firsthand and be warmly received into their homes during visitations. Because the clinic was charity-based, the numbers of patients coming to us was growing rapidly, and the midwives were delivering as many as five babies every day—requiring us to hire more midwives and host a growing number of foreign missionary volunteers.

For me personally, it took a while to reconcile my role as a male in this type of ministry and I found myself humbled by what I was witnessing. The favor the midwives were naturally gaining in the community was unprecedented compared to any other type of ministry I'd been involved in. Typical church planting strategy recommends looking for a *man of peace* in the community, bring him to Christ and seek to share the gospel through his web of relationships and influence. I realized a Christian midwife, to a limited extent, even though she may be new to the area, serves as a man of peace or in her case a *woman of peace* due to the nature of her services. Generally, if strangers from a church located outside of Agdao wanted to visit a family in the squatter communities, the husband typically jumped out the back window and disappeared into the neighboring house while his wife accommodated the visitors. However, each time *we* visited a patient's house the husband and wife warmly welcomed us because of the positive experience they enjoyed at the clinic. Furthermore, our midwife staff allowed the husbands to be present in the birthing room, which wasn't allowed at the local government hospital where as many as 40–60 babies were delivered every 24 hours. It wasn't uncommon to see a husband cry or become overjoyed when our midwives laid his new baby into his arms. The relational connection was initiated by the patients who came to the clinic, and incubated by the midwife who demonstrated God's kindness and compassion throughout the course of her pregnancy.

This nurturing relationship allowed the midwives to experience varying levels of immersion into the lives of hundreds of families. As they listened to their patients share stories of conflict it enabled us to accurately understand why the poor were so disadvantaged. A common thread inexorably woven amongst the life fabric of countless patients interviewed by the midwives was the injustices their husbands were subjected to by employers who cheated them out of their wages. The men were fearful of saying anything or reporting their employers to the Bureau of Labor because they knew the resulting retribution from the employer would be the immediate termination of their jobs, leaving them unable to provide for their families. The added fear that kept them from jeopardizing their employment was the cost for medical care. Every family lived on the precipice of financial devastation if a child needed hospitalization or expensive medicines, which doctors frequently prescribed in order to earn kickbacks from the pharmaceutical companies.

14.

Helping While Stumbling

It quickly became evident that opportunities for additional ministry programs were abundant. We tried to help families in very practical ways and determined one of the most helpful things we could do was to provide access to capital.

I discovered through trial and error that many people living in squatter communities, even if they had access to funds, would squander it. Trust and personal responsibility provide the framework of a value system based on integrity, and working with people lacking those values is both frustrating and disappointing, especially when you're sincerely trying to help them. Oftentimes people took advantage of us because we were Christians, and even more so because we were missionaries. For example, we would on occasion provide micro-loans with reasonable terms, some of which included zero interest loans. However, we found that getting people to repay was practically impossible and they made up all kinds of excuses to defer the scheduled payment. There's a difference between a reason and an excuse, and what we thought were legitimate reasons at the time were actually excuses.

One day I visited someone in their makeshift house located on a vacant lot where he had an arrangement with the owner to guard (*bantay*) it in order to keep squatters out. We were standing just inside the door when a man with a dark complexion suddenly rode up on his motorcycle and parked under a coconut tree. My friend immediately excused himself and advised that he'd only be a moment. I watched out of curiosity and noticed that although very few words were said between them, some money had been exchanged. Then the man mounted his motorcycle and took off as quickly as he'd arrived.

When my friend turned back inside he offered an explanation for what had just happened, although I hadn't inquired. He had borrowed money to buy a new karaoke system and told me that man was an Indian Boombay—a misnomer for the Indian city of Bombay—and pronounced "boom-bye," which is a slang term for an Indian Punjabi money lender. These people are actually Philippine citizens, descendants of 19th century Indian immigrants. Their primary business is to lend money to poor people who don't have access to other loans due to the lack of assets for collateral. The more popular term for these money lenders is "5/6" due to the terms of their lending model. A person borrows ₱5 pesos and repays ₱6, calculated on a daily basis and collected weekly. The loan payoff is usually limited to two to three months, which psychologically helps alleviate the sting of such an exorbitant interest rate—20%.

I was intrigued, not so much by the lending scheme, but by the fact the money lender was able to collect the scheduled payment without any objection or hesitation from my friend. I'd seen many 5/6 guys riding around town on their motorcycles and observed the interaction they had with their clients was very quick, usually a few brief moments. They were no-nonsense guys and fully expected to be paid when they showed up. I assumed these weekly meetings were scheduled and the person was expected to have the money ready to immediately turn over once the Boombay drove up.

I was fascinated as to the efficiency of the loan repayment so I asked a question, "What would happen if you didn't give the money to that Boombay?"

My friend replied, "He would have walked into my house and taken away my karaoke."

I followed with another question; "Why is it, then, when I loan money to help people it's very difficult to collect monthly payments, even when it's a small loan and I don't charge any interest?"

I was not expecting the answer I received.

"People don't repay you," he said, "because they know you're a Christian missionary and you will eventually forgive the debt because you feel sorry for them."

His response was a watershed moment for me.

113

Throughout those years we endured resounding failures and made so many mistakes trying to help people, mostly by omission, because we didn't grasp the depth of the problems facing these impoverished people. Furthermore, and more importantly, we fell short at understanding certain cultural issues regarding the economy of money, or we lacked sufficient training in implementing models that were already well-proven in other areas. Generally, each time we tried to help people I felt like that mechanic working at Starbucks. I had no idea how to make a Macchiato and I had no idea how to help these people.

* * *

Sometimes things completely slipped by our ability to rightly discern, like being duped by people and their stories. People must have laughed at our gullibility and we became a true-life example of its definition; "The tendency to believe unlikely propositions that are unsupported by evidence." I lost count of the number of opportunists who took full advantage of us. The following is a true story told by Gary, an American missionary, who served on our team along with his wife, Lynn, for seven years.

"After a considerable amount of time and money spent trying to help Boy and Lynette in everything from cottage industries, medical needs, jobs, etc., I began to (finally) suspect they were not on the level and began curtailing my help and ceased even spending time with them. After about three months with no interaction, [Boy] showed up at the clinic one day. I saw him maybe 100 feet away, just standing there incredibly distraught. Tears were running down his anguished face as he could hardly get the words out. I realized later it was an Academy Award winning performance. As the story went, Lynette had gone to Manila some time before to help care for her struggling mother. While there, she supposedly had a dizzy spell, fell over and hit her head on the concrete and died! As soon as he got word of what happened, he came to see if I would pay boat fare for him and the three kids to get to Manila. He wanted to get there quickly before the funeral was over and if he left the next morning, he would get there just in time.

"I loved these people in spite of their unfaithfulness and sketchy ways. I truly believed the story! He and his children were staying temporarily at a shelter so I went there to see if I could validate the story. Boy urged me not to speak of Lynette's passing in the children's presence, as he hadn't had the heart to break the news to them yet! Apparently, he had also given the same story to the people running the shelter. The director had suspicions and cautioned me not to give him any cold hard pesos, but instead suggested I buy the tickets personally and watch him get on the ship with my own eyes. I bought the tickets and returned to the shelter. Boy was not there, so I gave the tickets to the people in the office and arranged to pick Boy up the next morning bright and early and take them to the dock. The next morning they were gone—with the tickets. I raced to the docks and inquired as to whether they had boarded. The folks there assured me they thought he had, so I left feeling I'd done the right thing by not giving them any money.

"A week or so later, I was relating Lynette's death to some people in Agdao who had known her. One of the guys had been doing his bottle collecting (*bote bakal*) business in Panabo recently and thought he had seen Lynette sitting outside a shack drinking coffee. So we loaded up and made a trip to Panabo. We didn't find her or Boy, but the people in Panabo assured us that she was alive and well.

"So many things come into play in the 'Gullibility of the Missionary,' including the 'Great White Savior' complex. It feels good to be needed and to have the means to help. The 'Guilt Complex' develops when we consider the disparity in lifestyle and income between them and us. How can I say no? The western 'Let's fix this mindset. And then there is the

'Justify my existence here' complex. We want to help! We want to make a difference! We are compassionate! We were called to minister to the poor. Jesus lavished his love, mercy and grace upon us over and over! How can we do any less? What would Jesus have done? Still wash their feet? Still die for their sins, even knowing they were ripping him off? Suffice to say, all the lessons were valuable and ever so slowly, wisdom begins to temper and guide compassion."

Gary didn't elaborate on the unanswered issue regarding the tickets, but I'll surmise that Boy either sold the tickets to earn some quick cash or he simply kept the charade going in order to save face when he realized Gary wasn't going to give him the money. I once listened with laughter as another team member detailed how a total stranger had tricked him into buying infant milk formula for his baby girl and how elaborate the scheme evolved until it became so complex to the point where the missionary got lost in his ability to discern what was going on. In the end the guy got the money out of our team member who realized much later that he had fallen for a fantastic story that lacked any truth.

A kind elderly Filipino lady set us straight one day when she advised, "If you really want to know the truth about anyone's story just ask their neighbor." There are no secrets in squatter communities. Everyone knows everyone's dirty laundry.

* * *

We also made many cultural mistakes regarding communication styles. Filipinos generally avoid using overtly negative connotations such as saying "No" to someone, which Westerners generally won't hesitate to express. For a Filipino, it's even considered culturally inappropriate to say "I'm not interested." Instead, innuendo and inference is the preferred way to communicate regarding negative feedback, which any Filipino would certainly pick up on. Unfortunately, we lacked the depth to sufficiently understand many of the cultural nuances steeped in Filipino communication styles, which take years to appropriately discern. For example, we offered to help people with various ideas that *we* had envisioned, but failed to understand that by accepting the offer the recipient covers the loss of face the giver would experience if the recipient was hesitant or said "No thanks." In other words, the recipient was culturally bound to accept our offer in order to cover the possible shame we might feel if he rejected us.

It took years to understand how important it is, in our service as missionaries, to look through the contextual lens concerning the values, communication styles, and cultural forces in order to be effective—primary of which is understanding that "Honor–Shame" is an ever-present and deeply embedded force in Philippine culture.

In those days, we didn't have access to materials or books we could have studied regarding proven ways to help the poor. We were just guided by our gut feeling, assuming we were effectively making a difference by helping people. Our interpretation of how to help, which was usually motived by emotion, always defaulted to our assumption that financial or in-kind assistance would solve the problem. We were more inclined to reach into our wallet than consider any other option because it was easy to defer to the perceived power of money.

During the past decade, there have been multiple studies on the practicalities of helping the poor using various models. Unlike today where there is an abundance of resources to draw from on this subject, such as *When Helping Hurts* by Brian Fikkert and Steve Corbett who explain that we oftentimes undermine the people and communities we're trying to help because our approach is misguided—although well-intended. The paradigm that needs to be embraced is a focus on sustainable change from within people's hearts and from within their communities. "Inside-out rather than outside-in" as someone said.

Although transformation in varying degrees was often present within the community, the ability to experience sustainable impact is sometimes blocked by the very people you are trying to help because engagement and reconciliation are integral components of a sustainable model involving community development. A perfect example of this involved an outreach we undertook at a place called Water Lilly, a lower-class community with 20–30 houses situated on stilts over a freshwater lake about four hectares in size.

The community actually enjoyed the benefits of a healthy sustained ecosystem. Several families tended floating vegetable gardens that were supported by thick aquatic weed mats which serve as a base for growing vegetables. Some men caught fresh fish for their livelihood by using long electrical probes they inserted into the water that stunned the fish and caused them to float to the surface for easy retrieval.

We were having problems accessing the area where the midwives were conducting prenatal home visits for pregnant women. The primary route into Water Lilly was a narrow-dilapidated footbridge made from rotten boards attached to rickety stilts situated about four inches above the water line. Every attempt to walk across was precarious and an invitation to take a plunge with each step. A young woman who had gone into labor had to be carried out by several men who held her above their shoulders as they waded through the water rather than take a chance on using the wooden walkway.

We decided that repairing the footbridge would be a great community-service outreach. We approached the community and advised them of our plans, but their response wasn't what we had hoped. In fact, they seemed quite dismissive about the whole idea. I recalled the problems we'd encountered regarding the Aeta's unwillingness to help us with the school construction, and I observed this in other situations. It was very frustrating as a foreigner to continually experience a common thread of disengagement woven amongst people when it involved both community development and community service related projects. What we didn't know at the time was an underlying problem had been present in the community, which had nothing to do with our assumptions about the culture. Instead, it had everything to do with the hearts and attitudes of the people.

Frustration due to the lack of commitment and assistance from the community led us to act independently, purchasing the materials and fixing the walkway ourselves. Our justification seemed valid; pregnant women needed outside intervention in order to help them get access to maternal healthcare without the risk of ending up in a lake on their way to the clinic.

Just as we were about to start the project one of the community members approached us and said, "We have the ability to fix the walkway ourselves.

The problem isn't the money because we can collect all we need to pay for it as a community. The problem is that some hard headed (*bugoy*) people refuse to help and we believe everyone should be involved because every household uses the walkway. We've had several meetings to discuss this problem, which always lead to arguments. If you fix the boards (*kahoy*) then it will only make the situation worse because it will empower the hardheaded ones who refuse to help." Needless to say, we stopped working on the project.

* * *

A few times we got it right though, and one story in particular stands out as a true success. It's the kind of story that seemed small and insignificant but it transcended many previous mistakes and brought the presence of God into the life narrative of a young woman name Alma.

Paul advised Timothy to "invest in faithful men." I began to realize, after additional trial and error, that those four words were foundational and served as the baseline for helping people. Alma's husband earned about $3 per day as a tricycle driver and she worked part time for Krys and I, helping to clean the apartment. Alma had four children and when we didn't have enough work she tended to roam around the barangay, looking for ways to earn enough to help supplement her husband's meager daily income. I had observed Alma to be industrious, honest and hardworking. On more than one occasion she confided to me her desire to have her own business, but lacked the capital to get anything started.

One day I presented a proposal for her consideration. I read to her the *Parable of the Talents* from Matthew 25, which is the story Jesus told about a landowner who separately entrusted money to three servants before he left on a journey. The story relates what each servant did with the money, for which they were required to give an account when their master returned. Two were praised for doubling their money while the third was rebuked for burying it in the ground for safekeeping. It's a wonderful story about personal responsibility and faithfulness.

I explained to Alma that, with her permission, I'd like the two of us to act out that story. I offered to play the role of the master and she would be the servant. I was sensitive to the connotation implied by the word "master" as the landowner is referred to in the story so I kept emphasizing that we were only role playing. I then handed her ₱500, which at the time was about $20, and told her to do with it according to whatever was in her heart—with the condition that she was not to spend any of it on herself or her family. Instead, she was to return all the money to me, including any increase, exactly as Jesus narrated in His story.

Alma was both excited and a little nervous so I advised her to pray and ask God what she should do with my money, with the emphasis on "my." The next day she returned to my apartment and told me that she wanted to buy and sell eggs but admitted that she was scared of making a mistake and ending up like the foolish servant. I responded by telling her that most people fail because they lack the courage to even try.

I was very careful in my approach with Alma because I'd already made several mistakes in loaning money to people. Alma struggled with the business idea and didn't understand the mechanics of what was required, so I explained that she needed to find someone who would sell eggs to her at wholesale. Then I helped her figure out what the retail price point needed to be in order to make it worthwhile, taking into account her time and effort.

I was prepared to give Alma 30 days for us to try this little experiment, but five days later she returned to my house, exclaiming that she had completed her role as the faithful servant based on the parable. She had befriended an egg vendor in the public market (*palengke*) who agreed to sell her several dozen eggs at a discounted wholesale price, then she resold them to the owner of a local variety store (*sari-sari*)—a small family-run convenience store found in every neighborhood throughout the country.

With a huge smile, Alma unloaded her little purse and placed ₱1,000 on the table in front of me, most of which was a pile of small coins. She had doubled her money by buying and selling several dozen eggs! I decided to have a little fun with her and slid the entire pile of coins toward me and said, "Thanks." After a long pause, she asked why I got to keep all the money. I referenced the parable and reminded her that all the money was returned to the master, including the excess that had been earned from the two faithful servants. After another pause I continued, "The bible also says a workman is worthy of his hire and deserves his wages. And, you're not my servant, and I'm not your master."

I separated the initial ₱500 I entrusted to her then slid the other ₱500 back across the table to Alma. "Five days ago you had nothing," I said. "Now, you have your own ₱500, so you can use this as capital to keep your egg business going or come up with another idea." Alma was a simple-minded lady but that simple interaction had a profound impact on her because, as she related to me, that was the first time she experienced God in a real way. Furthermore, she had gone to all of her neighbors and testified what had happened, telling them she had lived out a bible story in real life. All I had done was invest in a faithful person and empowered her with capital to follow an idea she had come up with on her own.

15.

Social Ministry Tension

During a leadership meeting, after we'd been serving in Agdao for a few years, one of our team members voiced an inner conviction.

"If taking care of people is all we do then we should just join the Peace Corps or some other international relief agency," he said.

It was an honest comment I respected and understood, but it lacked the recognition of a larger context. We weren't limiting our efforts as a team to providing maternal healthcare and engaging in various community service projects at the exclusion of sharing our witness for Christ. Each of us recognized the importance evangelism needed to play in our ministry, which is the point the team member was trying to make. Charles Fielding wrote almost a decade later in his formative book *Preach and Heal* that "Mission history around the world has been replete with an unfortunate tension between evangelism and social ministry."

We were intentional in demonstrating the character of Christ through compassion-based ministry centered around the clinic where a short bible study was shared with the patients every day when we gathered them in the large waiting room—followed by praying for each patient privately at the conclusion of her check-up.

An ever-present reality that was difficult to reconcile, however, was how to follow up on thousands of patients. We were literally overwhelmed with a growing number of people coming to the clinic; as many as 120 patients every day. It was exhausting and we simply didn't have the time or ability to follow up on so many people—thus the "tension."

I've gained an important insight regarding the "preach-heal" thing while overseeing more than 200 missionaries who have served on our team during the past 20-plus years. It's simply this—not all *healers* are necessarily *preachers*, just as not all *preachers* are necessarily *healers*. The Great Commission provides a mandate to "Go" and the *Little Commission*—also given by Jesus as described in Matthew 10—says, "Heal the sick, raise the dead, cleanse the lepers, cast out demons." There's more to the Commission than preaching and healing. The outworking parts of the Great Commission aren't all-inclusive to every person individually as if they need to do everything themselves. It's like a vast canvas with many people serving in different areas with respect to their individual gifting. In our case, we were many parts, each exercising our respective gifts, all of which complemented the team as a whole. Some delivered babies, others did translation works, and some did administrative work, cooked meals, started music lessons to reach youth, or were involved in micro-lending. Still others did agricultural work, and some team members built deep relationships by faithfully visiting patient's families in their homes or simply introducing themselves to complete strangers and starting bible studies.

One of our former team members, Mordegai, who is from Namibia, South Africa, pioneered the primary healthcare component of our team ministry. He sought out people living at the lowest social levels who were suffering from various physical ailments. Generally, their possessions were quite sparse and they rented a bed space from someone, or they might collect pieces of cardboard that was tacked to a few pieces of scrap lumber, which served as makeshift walls for what might barely be classified as a house.

Mordegai spent hours walking around squatter communities, looking for people who needed help and often worked among the sea gypsies (*Badjaos*) living over the water in crude bamboo houses on stilts or living in their small boats. He bound up wounds, fed them, secured medicines, sought out free medical care from local doctors for the hard cases, and even remained by the side of people while they died.

Mordegai is best described as a man who is fully *"Wild at Heart"* as John Eldredge writes in his best-selling book, and he eventually tired of the urban setting because he knew that people living in the mountainous interior regions were in worse shape and needed his help. He bought a motorcycle, welded steel mounts to the frame to hold medical supplies then rode deep into remote areas in order to help as many people as he could. After sundown, he would show *The Jesus Movie* using a video projector and a small portable generator.

It didn't take for long for Mordegai to realize the single greatest physical ailment people suffered from, more so than any other health issue, was rotting teeth. A visiting American dentist offered to train him how to pull teeth, which was the only option for people living that remote. Mordegai kept meticulous details and I recall him mentioning that he'd pulled 7,000 teeth during one year alone.

* * *

I likened our experience managing the team during the first several years to a pair of train tracks running parallel to each other. One track represented the challenges of overseeing a multinational team. The Filipino Christian midwives and support staff were all wonderful people who really enjoyed working at the clinic. Our Filipino staff walked us through many situations and very patiently helped us understand the problems endemic to impoverished families. They also guided us as we worked with various government officials, whether it was at the local barangay level or with the national government such as the Department of Health or the Department of Social Welfare and Development.

The adjacent track involved our attempts to get the foreign team members from the United States and Canada on the same page with the overall team and provide direction and oversight for them. There are vast differences between the autonomous, individualistic "Guilt–Innocence" culture of the west and the collective "Honor–Shame" culture of Asia. Much to our advantage, the Filipino people as a society are incredibly long-suffering and patient when it comes to conflict or misunderstanding. Rarely did we experience conflict with the staff, but at times we experienced misunderstandings caused by us as foreigners immersed into another culture with values and forces that conflicted with those of the west. The Filipinos consistently met us more than halfway in minimizing those misunderstandings, meaning they would be the ones to demonstrate grace and patience toward us, even though we should have been the ones to capitulate since we were the guests in their country. The problem was that we often didn't recognize when we made the mistake, and the Filipinos by nature don't tend to point out errors or missteps, which embraces the cultural value of maintaining honor in relationships at all costs.

* * *

The primary challenge Krys and I struggled to manage as the leaders during those early years was the fact that our team was somewhat dynamic in the sense that it had a high turnover of Westerners. The 200 missionaries I've referred to who have joined us over the years have come for varying lengths of time. Some have come for 6-12 months, but most commit for 2-year terms while a few have served longer—up to 7 years. Initially, during the first few years, new people were staying for only 6 months and they lacked sufficient context or continuity regarding our history—knowledge of which would have enabled them to understand what we were trying to do as leaders directing a team.

Unfortunately, some of the short-term people had their own agendas and felt led to do what they believed was right, which stemmed from their "wealth." They were the "haves" and wanted to help the "have-nots." In retrospect, and this is difficult to admit, I think some of our motives came from the feeling that helping disadvantaged people felt empowering, and having that feeling of dominance was something new to our Western team members.

"It feels good to be needed," as Gary wrote, which fed the *Great White Savior* complex. I distinctly recall one particular story involving a short-term twenty-something American female team member who visited a patient at her squatter home. The patient's husband was present and when she learned that he didn't have any work she pulled a ₱1,000 bill out of her pocket and dropped it on the table in front of them, believing she'd demonstrated an act of amazing compassion.

During orientation for all new arrivals, we cautioned people regarding money and advised that we shouldn't necessarily default to giving out cash to people. We explained that God hadn't called us to the country to hand out money, and it had been our experience that doing so was actually counter-productive to our ministry. For example, we learned the community as a whole would collectively make provision for a safety net regarding urgent and legitimate issues that were presented such as a medical emergency, or if a family lacked money for food. I've witnessed money literally come out of the woodwork where people had kept it hidden when a neighbor has a medical emergency. Or if someone in the community didn't have food, a neighbor would share a meal. The recipient of that assistance then becomes obligated to the donors via a cultural binder known as *utang* (indebtedness) which compels families to help one another because everyone is indebted to everyone else.

One of the hardest lessons I learned, which really grieved me, was listening to someone explain the negative effect we were having in the community each time we provided money or in-kind help to people in need. I learned to listen carefully when a Filipino from the community took the time to counsel or advise us. He explained when a missionary offers financial assistance the community tends to pull back the safety net, feeling they no longer need to help one another during a crisis. Their perspective is, "Why should we help a family in need when the missionary will do it? We're having a difficult time just trying to take care of our own."

I tried to explain to the young lady who dropped the money on the table that she had inadvertently shamed the husband in front of his wife and caused him to lose face in the eyes of his neighbors once they learned what happened. She had misinterpreted what they were communicating to her during the home visit because they hadn't asked for a handout. Instead, they were just sharing their story and perhaps hoping we might be able to refer them if we knew of a job opening somewhere. Too many times, we failed to bring God into the situation and simply pray for the family. Instead, we took on the role of God and provided for them out of our own pocketbooks.

Granted, these few stories don't necessarily shine a light on everything involved in helping impoverished families, which can be incredibly complex. Thankfully, today there are a multitude of excellent books that provide a wealth of experience and advice regarding how to effectively introduce sustainable change to communities.

Krys and I tended to shy away from implementing policies to govern the team because we believed that once a policy manual is introduced then it becomes the default management mechanism based on a static set of rules. Granted, policies and guidelines are needed for HR management of a company including the larger mission organizations, but rarely do policy manuals make sufficient provision for flexibility, and the very nature of our ministry required enormous flexibility. We avoided policies that mandated what people could and could not do and trusted they would respect our leadership and honor what we were asking of them.

Unfortunately, we hosted several people over the years who were entirely resistant to any input or direction. I likened it to drilling a hole in a piece of sheet metal, which I had learned to do in my 8th grade Industrial Arts class. A drill bit spinning at any rpm will wander around the surface of that metal and never bite the steel if you don't tap a guide divot. Some people who joined our team wandered all over the place just like a spinning drill bit. They had their own expectation and opinion of how cross-cultural ministry should be done, despite having zero experience. They gave cash to the poor without our knowledge even after we asked them not to do it, and they wouldn't seek our advice before doing something we had already experienced and knew wouldn't work.

Some people simply didn't want anyone to guide them and I realized it had nothing to do with our leadership style. I'll admit it was messy at times and those people exacerbated the challenges of overseeing the evolution of a cohesive team. John Maxwell said "everything rises and falls on leadership." I realize he's a bestselling author, but in my experience of leading a mission team I will state unequivocally that everything does not rise and fall on leadership. Followers, whether they are employees, volunteers, team members, interns, etc., always make up the other half of the equation. Together, leaders and followers both have an obligation to act as stewards of the organization. Both have a vested interest with a mutually beneficial outcome.

Maxwell also said that "leaders need to preserve the integrity of the organization." Again, I'll turn the focus on the follower because the integrity of the follower is also crucial to enabling the leader to fulfill his role—as it relates to a volunteer-based mission team. A follower's lack of integrity can be severely detrimental to the integrity of the mission organization. Krys and I have been in situations where we were forced to go to incredible lengths, which cost us dearly, in order to salvage the extensive damage wrought by another team member. It had nothing to do with leadership.

Three things I've learned over the years. First, serving alongside people who walk in integrity and take ownership in the ministry is the most fulfilling and rewarding experience a leader can enjoy. Second, dealing with people who aren't teachable is like gargling with vinegar. Third, some people just prefer to do their own thing and wander around like a drill bit doing the waltz on steel, even when leadership has placed a divot for them to bite into and make a difference. Some people can't help but hijack their own experience, and at times they hijack the organization, forcing leadership to make difficult decisions or engage on a level they prefer not to, in order to preserve the integrity of organization.

Despite the challenges, which no leader or organization is immune to experiencing, we saw God's hand and provision on the ministry. Isaiah 58 became a predominant theme in our work and I oftentimes brought it to the Lord in prayer and witnessed God honoring His promise to be our "rear guard" and answering us when we called because we were helping the disadvantaged and poor.

> Is not this the kind of fasting I have chosen:
> Is it not to share your food with the hungry
> and to provide the poor wanderer with shelter—
> when you see the naked, to clothe them,
> Then your light will break forth like the dawn,
> and your healing will quickly appear;
> then your righteousness will go before you,
> and the glory of the Lord will be your rear guard.
> Then you will call, and the Lord will answer;
> you will cry for help, and he will say: Here am I.
> And if you spend yourselves in behalf of the hungry
> and satisfy the needs of the oppressed,

then your light will rise in the darkness,
 and your night will become like the noonday.
The Lord will guide you always;
 he will satisfy your needs in a sun-scorched land
and will strengthen your frame.
 You will be like a well-watered garden. (Is: 58:6-11 NIV)

16.

Train & Multiply

As much as the varying ministry efforts of the team members were bearing fruit—all of which served as a framework for what I believed was a holistic ministry model—I wanted to be involved in church planting. I had devoured several books by authors who wrote extensively about missiological church planting such as C. Peter Wagner, Roland Allen, Charles Brock who wrote *The Indigenous Church*, Robert E. Logan, Dick Scoggins, and others. These authors helped me understand that "Church planting is the most effective evangelistic methodology under heaven" as Wagner said. The interest to be involved in church planting grew from my own personal desire, yet with the hope that everyone on the team might feel they were also being represented in that arena—just as I and the other men on the team were being represented by the midwives serving the patients.

We were able to start a few home bible studies and saw some people baptized, and we did our best to disciple them. We also started an informal church that met in the clinic every Saturday evening, which was loosely modeled on Rick Warren's book *The Purpose Driven Church*. Approximately 80 people attended each service—most of whom were from the nearby squatter community. Running those services was a team effort and took a lot of work, but after three months I realized the stress of managing the church added to the workload of the staff, primarily the national midwives. One day I found two of our midwives hiding in one of the birth rooms and was grieved when I heard them tell me honestly that they just couldn't continue to help with the church in addition to taking care of 80–100 patients each day. I realized this massive workload was costing us, and as the leader I knew we were literally wearing out our staff by asking them to be both midwives and pastors—*healers* and *preachers*. It wasn't a church model that could be sustained, and at that point I realized it was time to implement Patterson's strategy, which I'd put on pause until it was translated into the local dialect.

Dr. Patterson had previously explained to me the basic precepts of the strategy, but it all came together once I was able to personally review and carefully study the materials, which I had hand-carried with me to Mindanao. The strategy and accompanying curriculum is called *Train and Multiply*, which is a reformatted and compiled version of the hundreds of small booklets Dr. Patterson created while serving as a field missionary. He donated his materials to SEAN (Study by Extension for All Nations) when he left the mission field, and SEAN, together with a team of people that included Dr. Patterson, spent years editing and condensing his original manuals into 60 booklets plus supportive teaching guides and came up with the *Train and Multiply* (T&M) name.

It took us two years to translate T&M into the Philippine Visayan dialect with the help of a full-time Filipino lady whom we hired to translate the materials and make sure it was properly formatted for printing. When Level One was completed I introduced it to two Filipino pastors, Pastor Saniel and Pastor Bobong, who were working in a remote provincial area and had stressed a genuine interest in implementing the strategy after I spent time explaining it during several visits. Initially, I was inclined to observe the results of a trial run and was obviously curious to see if T&M was effective for training lay people as Patterson had claimed.

After several weeks, Pastor Saniel and Pastor Bobong reported that a couple of new students whom they enrolled in the T&M program were working in a remote mountainous region and had successfully started informal bible studies after seeing people embrace Christ. I was very encouraged by the progress these two pastors were having during the following months, and to some degree, even on a small scale, I determined the results were measurable and consistent with what Patterson had experienced and taught.

* * *

About six months later I met Kenny Wong, an Asian-American missionary, whose mission organization worked collaboratively with DAWN (Disciple a Whole Nation). DAWN was an incredibly successful movement that brought together representatives of every Philippine Christian denomination and para-church organization, pledging unprecedented cooperation to make sure each of the country's 44,000 barangays had a church. The vision was cast and an important framework was laid out to provide the necessary components to help DAWN move forward, which included collecting data and mobilizing people to plant new churches.

From this proposal, the "Philippines DAWN 2000 Movement" was formally organized which allowed each denomination and para-church organization to act autonomously in setting its own goals and establishing the infrastructure to accomplish the vision laid out by DAWN.

Kenny took the time to explain how DAWN was organized and told me their organization was heavily vested in the research side of the strategy. One of their Filipino team members, Chris Balaga, was DAWN's nationally appointed head researcher, whose job was to coordinate and mobilize a small army to visit every barangay in the country and gather data regarding the number of represented churches, and identify which barangays lacked any church presence. Supplemental data was also collected such as contact information of the pastors, the church size, membership, which churches hadn't formally organized, those lacking a full-time pastor, etc.

The collected data was then disseminated to the denominations and independent organizations, which prompted a collaborative goal to mobilize church planters to those barangays lacking a church. It had been discovered that accurate data on a national scale provided an important motivational factor. For example, the researchers might report that a particular region had 332 churches scattered amongst 183 barangays, but 70 of those barangays didn't have a single church. Subsequently, churches in the adjacent barangays committed to mobilizing people and working towards establishing a new church in the barangays that lacked a church presence.

* * *

It soon became evident there was an obvious limitation; bible schools weren't producing enough graduates to plant the number of churches needed to fulfill DAWN's target—a church in every barangay. At the time 30,000 barangays lacked an evangelical church presence, and the average bible school was producing less than 10 graduates per year.

Kenny heard about *Train and Multiply* and upon request, someone in the UK had mailed him a few sample copies of the individual training booklets, but he didn't have enough of the materials to understand how it worked. When Kenny explained to me there was a coordinated national strategy involved, I showed him the complete set of T&M materials I had spent two years translating. I explained how it was designed to serve as a curriculum that senior pastors could use to train their lay leaders how to plant daughter churches under their direct oversight.

Kenny and I worked hard to create a seminar format, which followed an active learning model, in order to help us demonstrate important things necessary for pastors to understand how to implement the T&M training program in their churches. In addition, we were committed to providing a copy of the entire curriculum to each pastor who attended our seminars if they reimbursed us for the reproduction cost—about $10. We had purchased a high speed Risograph machine capable of producing high volume copies, and two girls working full-time produced three million individual pages of the materials, which were collated into thousands of complete curriculum sets, available in English or the Visayan dialect. Tagalog, Ilocano, and other translations were produced later.

For the next two years we traveled throughout the country, training pastors a New Testament model for church planting and equipping them with the T&M pastoral training materials. We also had the privilege of having Chris Balaga accompany us to several of our training workshops, and it was fascinating to witness the level of interest and cooperation amongst the pastors who were members of city or provincial ministerial fellowships.

Chris would provide current data regarding DAWN's progress, which was an update on how the national goal was progressing. He always brought large maps copied onto poster size sheets of cartolina paper which he attached to the walls with adhesive tape. The maps displayed a mark representing every church in the barangays from the region of those attending. For example, when we conducted a workshop for the pastoral association located in Agusan del Norte, Chris had maps prepared displaying the demographic divisions of that region; 166 barangays spread throughout 12 municipalities. The maps highlighted which barangays had a church witness and those lacking any church presence.

After we completed a T&M seminar, Chris would invite the pastors to pray for a few moments and then step forward to sign their name in one of the empty spaces on the maps representing a barangay without a church. I watched in amazement as pastors and their lay leaders stepped forward with a resolute commitment to plant a new church in the barangays that lacked any evangelical presence. We respectfully helped them grasp the importance and validity of church multiplication, how to evangelize and disciple new believers, and how to implement an on-the-job pastoral training program within their church. Then we provided them with a complete set of the materials translated into their dialect.

At the end of those two years we had trained over 10,000 pastors and lay leaders, representing every denomination in the Philippines. Although the DAWN strategy was national in scope we were playing a small role in mobilizing indigenous church planters and Christian workers by using a proven and effective strategy amongst other strategies being employed around the country.

* * *

Ironically, that wonderful experience also exposed me to some deep-rooted Western-based paradigms that were counter-productive to the concept of church multiplication we were trying to encourage. DAWN was a dead-end vision if churches didn't multiply and plant daughter churches. The T&M curriculum emphasized that it was important to distinguish between New Testament commands—such as baptism—and human traditions, which can actually hinder obedience to Christ. Some pastors were highly resistant to the idea of empowering theologically uneducated lay leaders to plant daughter churches. This, however, is a human tradition and not taught as a New Testament command.

We tried to be creative and used various analogies to help overcome some of the underlying traditions, which on a larger scale, were actually hindering DAWN from being successful. Our seminars were intended to be informal and we taught out-of-the-box using games, pictures, stories, role playing, etc. in order to help people experientially learn more than what they would endure in a typical lecture-based seminar where someone talks at them for eight hours.

To help build a bridge and validate the need for formally trained senior pastors to consider using lay leaders to plant new churches, we asked participants to role play the true story of Priscilla and Aquila's encounter with Apollos in Ephesus as recorded in Acts 18. That story represents a simple New Testament example of on-the-job training. Priscilla and Aquila stood to the side of the small crowd and listened attentively to what Apollos was preaching and noticed he was deficient in his understanding. Despite his error, they didn't interrupt or attempt to discredit Apollos, claiming he was unqualified to preach publicly because he didn't have all his facts straight, nor did they advise him to enroll in theology classes or get a bible school diploma before resuming his public ministry. Rather, they patiently waited until he was finished and then invited him for an iced cappuccino at a corner coffee shop where they provided him with a deeper explanation of the Christian faith, just as they had learned it from their time with Paul. Verse 26 says, "But when Priscilla and Aquila heard him, they took him aside and explained to him the way of God more accurately." Interestingly, a few days after their coffee meeting the narrative tells us that Apollos powerfully refuted the Jews by demonstrating through the scriptures that Jesus was the Christ.

We explained to pastors that the best incubator for effective on-the-job pastoral training was the local church rather than a static bible school or seminary. In effect, by using on-the-job training the senior pastor was actually the one planting the new church but he was doing it through the lay leaders in training who were under his direct oversight. Rather than being focused on growing his one church—as most pastors tend to do—we helped pastors understand they were expanding the fruit of their ministry by planting a daughter church, which would be an extension of the main church. We were careful to emphasize there is always an educated pastor on the Paul side of the Paul-Timothy link who was overseeing the new church by extension.

The role playing and other examples we used helped us qualify the importance of church multiplication, which enabled pastors to embrace the strategy and implement the curriculum. A very simple analogy seemed to have the best effect to help some resistant pastors grasp the importance of multiplication. During our seminars we'd project a picture of a large mango tree on the screen and ask, "What is the true fruit of a mango tree?" They always replied, "A mango." When we explained the mango fruit held the genetic code within the seed for another mango tree they realized the true fruit is actually another mango tree. From there we helped them understand the true fruit of their church isn't limited to another member being added to their membership role. Rather, it's another church and the members held the genetic code to *grow* another church.

It was fascinating to witness pastors rethink their paradigms and realize that each church member could be involved in ministry including training faithful lay leaders to start new churches. Granted, there's far more to the training than simply letting unqualified lay people go out and try to start a new church. T&M's strategy is well laid out and the training is very supportive and comprehensive.

* * *

I kept observing an intriguing pattern that became evident during our seminars. Pastors who had a background in business easily understood the multiplication proposal, because they related it to the business model of franchising. Pastors predisposed to being entrepreneurial-minded tended to question why things are done the way they've always been done, and they aren't afraid to go against the majority in order to make changes. In addition, they displayed a high amount of initiative, and we saw the most fruit with these pastors. They had a hard time working within the bureaucratic constraints of denominations and just preferred to work autonomously and be decisive. I applauded the denominational leaders who recognized this and were able to affirm those pastors with an entrepreneurial gifting. However, I also witnessed some denominational leaders suppress the gifting of these entrepreneurial people and stifle their ability to oversee reproducing churches. In fact, on a few occasions our workshops solicited some heated exchanges from pastors who felt constrained by their denominations. During one seminar I hosted in Cebu City the exchange became so bad that the pastors started arguing with each other. I felt for them and understood that a paradigm shift within the denominations needed to happen if DAWN was going to reach their target goals. The denominational leaders were godly men, but the idea to train lay leaders without requiring three to four-year residency bible school training was a real stretch for some of them.

I recall an independent non-denominational pastor coming to the office several months after attending one of our workshops in order to get additional copies of the *Train and Multiply* curriculum because he needed to train more lay leaders. He was very much an entrepreneurial ministry leader. When asked if he'd been able to plant any new churches using the materials, he told us that his students in training had been able to plant ten new churches. To hear a pastor tell us he'd planted ten churches was quite significant, and then we asked, "How did you plant ten churches?" He just looked at us and responded matter-of-factly, "I just did what you taught me at the workshop and followed the T&M strategy."

* * *

One day a denominational leader asked if I'd consider providing an overview of the T&M materials at a local bible school. He was familiar with the strategy and understood the curriculum was designed to be implemented as an extension of a local church and not a seminary. I did my best to decline and explained the workshop and materials were not compatible to being taught in a seminary setting, and doing so may very well backfire.

"It's a conflict of interest," I explained because I was familiar with that particular seminary and knew their model was a three-year residency program with minimal practical training.

"That seminary is using an outdated model and it's on life support," he replied. "The school is not going to make it if we don't introduce a new model to train students."

So, I asked, "Are you prepared for the ramifications because the faculty is most likely not going to appreciate it."

He said that he'd deal with the faculty if I agreed to teach the materials during an all-day workshop. I agreed when he told me that a private donor had offered to buy a complete set of T&M materials for each student.

The venue was a conference hall on campus that seated about 30 students, and much to my surprise the entire faculty was seated in the back row. I was informed they had actually been compelled to attend and didn't have a choice in the matter. I'd taught enough seminars to have a pretty good idea what to expect and I was intentionally respectful of the faculty's presence. Everything about T&M speaks to empowering lay leaders, and these faculty members lived in a paradigm wrapped in formal education being the primary avenue to train people for ministry. The students enjoyed the seminar and they had fun participating in role playing and a few games I used to help explain some pertinent points.

I opened the floor for questions toward the end of the day and was taken aback when a student stood up and said, "I'm a third-year resident getting ready to graduate and I can't believe they let you come in here and teach this material."

His candor was highly unusual because Filipinos are rarely that direct and candid. I didn't know what to say and initially thought he was going to challenge the strategy and much of what I had taught. I really had no desire to engage him in defending the strategy because I'd already had reservations about the presentation in a formal seminary anyway.

He continued, "Everything you've taught us today makes sense. I've been here three years and nothing they've trained me for compares to this strategy you've explained, particularly the idea of letting lay leaders plant churches. I feel like I've wasted three years of my life."

I was dumbfounded, not so much by the directness of his statement but at knowing the entire faculty—his professors—were sitting in the back row and clearly heard what he had expressed. I took the low road and answered a few more questions before I excused myself and left.

Several years later the person who invited me to speak at that seminary took over as the head of that school and started a *Seminary by Extension* modeled on the TEEE program using a combination of T&M, T4T (Training for Trainers) and materials he personally developed. Today, over 1,000 students are enrolled in extension classes while studying under the direct supervision of pastors in rural and urban churches.

* * *

Someone estimated over 1,000 churches had been planted as a result of the seminars we conducted. However, I landed on a more conservative number because it's very difficult to follow up on what was happening in the remote provincial areas.

We had also intentionally trained Filipino pastors how to conduct the seminars because we wanted to see nationals training nationals rather than us as foreign missionaries remaining in the forefront. These pastors traveled with us and listened carefully to how we taught the seminars. They believed in what we were teaching and personally witnessed fruit when their own churches successfully planted daughter churches using lay leaders.

After three years of full commitment to T&M, I determined it was time to pass the baton and let these Filipino pastors take the lead and conduct all the seminars. Also, a new door had opened for Kenny and his family to relocate to one of the Central Asian "stan" countries and he ended up leaving the Philippines.

It wasn't too long after stepping back from my involvement with T&M that I prayerfully turned my attention to something else that had been affecting me. Teenagers near the clinic in Agdao were being placed on hit lists and targeted for murder.

17.

Death Squads

Although we lived in the community, we were very much an enigma in Agdao because people were intrigued that Americans chose to live in Barrio Patay regardless of the fact we were missionaries. We were, therefore, to a limited degree considered insiders yet we remained very much as outsiders. We were constantly watched everywhere we went, whether it was walking down the street or buying vegetables in the market, but not in a bad light or disrespectful way. Rather, people were just transfixed by the fact we were white skinned people living in their community. We likened it to living inside a giant fishbowl.

As is probably common anywhere in the world, it was the children and teenagers who were the most intrigued and they would attempt to engage us, more so than the adults. I think they were motivated mostly by curiosity and their interest to be near us as foreigners whom they could practice their English on. I recall being shocked one day when a young boy who was probably around the age of five ran out of his house when he saw me walking from the clinic to my apartment and proceeded to tell me every American curse word he'd learned from watching pirated American videos. Then he turned around and ran back inside.

"Istambay" is a Filipino term taken from an American phrase; on stand-by. This was the typical response I received whenever I would engage teenagers living in Agdao and ask "How are you?" or "What are you doing today?" They'd often reply "istambay" which means "nothing" or "there's nothing to do." They're on stand-by, waiting for what will probably end up being nothing. The term wasn't just an excuse for not going out and finding a job or going to college after graduating high school. Either their families lacked enough money to enroll them in college or there simply weren't enough jobs in the marketplace for kids after they graduated from high school at the age of 15. This created a vulnerable time for them, and many were easily influenced by sexual experimentation and drawn into various vices such as drugs, alcohol and gambling. Unfortunately, fatalism and a resignation of the status quo bred a lot of passivity amongst many teenagers living in the squatter areas. Sadly, it becomes part of the fabric that shaped their future, which reinforced a sense of hopelessness. It was also evident their fathers had been pulled into the same vices years earlier, which helped numb the reality of poverty and dampen the guilt of not being able to provide for their families. Subsequently, there was no mentoring for many of the youth and the generational cycle repeated itself.

Several of the teens found themselves in trouble with the law due to petty crimes such as vandalism, theft and misdemeanors. Their legal liability was limited because they were minors, but it became entirely evident that it was only a matter of time until some of the youth were headed towards more serious problems, including being killed. Some of the teenage boys who hung around the clinic confided to us their fear of being added to the notorious DDS (Davao Death Squad) hit list.

* * *

The DDS is a vigilante group that carries out summary executions of criminals and drug dealers including youth involved in criminal behavior. One mother witnessed three of her teenage sons killed by the DDS due to their involvement in petty crimes. To date, according to the media, over 1,000 people have been executed in the city by masked hit men (*tirradors*) riding unregistered motorcycles who shoot the target as they slowly drive by. In order to send a message to other criminals, the executions are usually done during daytime and in public places with numerous witnesses.

There's a lot of ambiguity involving the mechanics of how the DDS operated, but the public knew the killings weren't random. Apparently, people on the list were privately watched to see if in fact they were guilty of committing crimes or pushing drugs. Prior to being murdered, many were given strong warnings to change their ways. People on the list, which was published and publicly disseminated, were given the option to turn themselves in to the police and submit to proper legal action or get out of town permanently.

The mayor of Davao, Rodrigo "Rody" Duterte, was featured on the cover of TIME magazine Asian edition, which referred to him as "The Punisher." He'd been called the "Dirty Harry" of the Philippines because he had zero tolerance for crime in his city and referred to criminals as societal garbage. Although people weren't personally connecting his involvement with the DDS, various international organizations such as the UN Human Rights Council criticized him for not doing anything to stop the group. Ironically, public opinion overwhelmingly supported the mayor because they witnessed a huge decline in crime that dropped from triple-digits per 1,000 to less than 10 per 1,000—all of which has been credited to the mayor and the DDS.

Duterte is an articulate person and his sayings have been widely published. His statement, which human rights advocates used to connect him to the DDS was; "If you are doing an illegal activity in my city, if you are a criminal or part of a syndicate that preys on the innocent people of the city, for as long as I am the mayor, you are a legitimate target of assassination." He also said, "Criminals do not have a monopoly on violence. If you are violent to the people of my city, then I will be violent to you. If you sell drugs to destroy other people's lives," he threatened, "I can be brutal."

A few legends have also arisen regarding Duterte, such as the claim he threw a top-level drug pusher out of a helicopter after storming his mountain hideout with the Army to arrest him. As the story goes, the drug pusher mocked Duterte while they were flying back to the airport and arrogantly assured the mayor he would never be convicted because he would just pay off the judge. In response, Duterte supposedly opened the door and pushed him out at 3,000 feet.

People find it difficult to overcome his reasoning and governance policies. Davao is the only city in the Philippines with a smoking ban—to protect non-smokers—and a ban on fireworks to prevent the noise from being used as a cover for gunfire. When the firecracker ban was implemented, Chinese-Filipino businessmen met with Duterte to ask if he would temporarily suspend the ban during the Chinese New Year. They claimed firecrackers frightened away evil spirits and they needed to set them off in order to protect their homes and businesses. Duterte's colorful response was, "No need to worry about the evil spirits. They won't bother you because I've already spoken to them and told them to leave town."

After a decade of taking decisive and strong action against criminals, the city's crime rate dropped so dramatically that tourism organizations dubbed it "one of the most peaceful cities in Southeast Asia." Even taxi drivers wouldn't think of cheating a passenger, lest he be publicly excoriated by Duterte in front of the media. A taxi driver once demanded I pay him more than what the meter showed by making up some reason for the extra fee. I wrote down his license number and replied that I'd be happy to pay what he was asking, but I'd report him directly to the mayor. The color drained from his face and he gladly let me pay the meter rate then quickly drove away. Davao was transformed into the "Jewel of the South" as people now refer to it, and it was voted as the "Most Livable City in the Philippines" and the third most livable city in all of Asia.

In 2016, Duterte went on to become the country's 16th president in a landslide election after promising an all-out brutal war on criminals. The month before he took office he announced that he was placing a bounty on all drug lords and drug pushers in the country, clarifying the bounty was payable if anyone on the list was brought in dead or alive. He encouraged those who were friends, neighbors, and relatives of dealers and abusers to turn them in to the police. Thousands of people all over the country voluntarily turned themselves into the regional police stations even before he officially took office. Duterte promised to get those who surrendered into rehabilitation programs, while those who didn't would be harshly dealt with. Surprisingly, within his first 6 months as the new president more than 1,000,000 drug dealers and users voluntarily surrendered to the police. Unfortunately, however, the country was plunged into a nightmare of summary killings of thousands—some of which were attributed to the police. Shoot to kill orders were placed on corrupt mayors who were protecting drug dealers, several of whom were killed in shootouts with the police. I believe history will judge his approach as detrimental to the country in the long run because other countries have tried similar methods and failed miserably.

* * *

But it was 1999, well before the city's transformation had taken place a decade later and very few ministries were at work in Agdao. YWAM was doing some outreaches in the area and a missionary couple from New Zealand, Phil and Judy McLean, started a school education sponsorship program targeting families who couldn't afford to buy knapsacks, shoes, basic school supplies or even pay the ₱2 pedicab fare to send their kids to the free public schools.

It's been said that a missionary becomes effective after he's been on the field for at least seven years. Obviously that's arguable, but I do think it takes several years to fine-tune our ability to rightly discern, and work out our egos and our know-it-all perceptions to where we can start discerning what God wants to do through us. We also learn by experience that just because an opportunity for ministry presents itself that doesn't necessarily mean God is in it. I've watched many missionaries embrace those opportunities as a mother hen gathers her chicks, only to see them exasperated later on as they tried to manage everything. In the end, all they did was expend a lot of energy and time with minimal results.

* * *

I had interacted with many youth from the barangay, some of whom would just hang out near the clinic because they longed for interaction with anyone who would give them some attention. Inviting a youth to church so people can preach at him was not working with the local churches that struggled to draw these kids into their youth groups. Campus Crusade for Christ had a very effective ministry at the local campuses, but they had trained staff members targeting college students who had a purpose in life and could afford tuition, unlike the troubled youth wandering around Agdao who lacked any purpose beyond the cycle of poverty that oftentimes hamstrung their ability to take a higher road.

I've watched or heard that missionaries sometimes try to solve people's lives, which I think comes from the false belief that we can fix the problems of other people. Each time I tried to approach ministry from that perspective it never worked. I don't think that's what God calls us to. I believe a fruitful ministry introduces people to God by testifying of His goodness and leading them to a personal experience with Him. Ministering God's compassion and mercy to a pregnant woman, for example, when she's never been offered such care is a relevant demonstration of the character of God's kingdom and His presence; especially when the only alternative is delivering her baby in the government hospital where she is one of 50 other women also in labor, and no one is getting individualized attention. She is also subjected to scolding, lectures, yelling and rough treatment from resident doctors overwhelmed with as many as 100 births in a 48-hour shift.

I wanted to introduce the youth to Christ in a way that was relevant, and I was fully confident we could effectively impact these kids if we could just extract them from their environment and drop them into a setting where they could become vulnerable and challenged to a point where they would long to embrace Christ. The idea I had was to immerse them into an adventure unlike anything they had ever experienced. For seven years, ever since Krys and I first arrived in the country, I often recalled an experience I'd had while living in Oklahoma during my early twenties when I participated in a specialized program called a ropes challenge course.

A ropes course involves using a series of ropes or cables featuring a variety of challenges designed to promote personal development and team building activity. The course typically consists of low elements situated on the ground, and high elements attached 10 – 20 feet off the ground using trees or utility poles. As part of the team building, participants learn to trust others on their team while working through the various elements.

That experience had a lasting impact on me, not necessarily because of the personal and team building challenges presented to the group I was with, but because I was immersed into a unique gospel presentation. Although each member of the group was already a Christian, the Christian facilitator took the opportunity to show us how he used the high and low elements to demonstrate an experiential way to share the gospel with people. I was fascinated.

I'd done a lot of research and found no evidence that ministries were using a ropes course to intentionally share the gospel message on the mission field. Youth, regardless of any culture or country they're from, respond to their environment and are influenced by the people and voices that comprise a sphere of social impressions. Removing a young person from what influences them presents an opportunity, if there is a concerted effort, to transcend those influences and immerse them into a new way of thinking. That may sound a bit too psychological, but here it is in a nutshell. Telling a youth that he needs Jesus is generally not going to be received at the level we'd hope due to the lack of context or application. Of course, I'm not implying such an approach limits the work of the Holy Spirit. Immersing a teenager into an environment and situations that mirror what he's dealing with in real life and letting him see how Christ desires to walk with him through his personal challenges is very impacting. They gain a sense of meaning, value and worth. He or she becomes incredibly vulnerable.

I wondered why challenge courses were not being considered as a viable tool for effective youth ministry because there is power in vulnerability. I believed that trained facilitators using a ropes course could effectively bring youth to a place of personal vulnerability, not by way of coercion or manipulation, but by making them feel safe enough to express themselves so we could talk to their hearts rather than dealing with the outward guises of everything a youth hides behind as he struggles to manage his life.

In his book *Experiencing God*, Henry Blackaby encourages Christians to "Find where God is working and join Him there." Unfortunately, there were no adventure-based challenge programs in the city—or in the entire country for that matter—where I could see God at work, which I could join. In fact, Filipinos for the most part had not yet been introduced to adventure-based programs, aside from a few guys who hiked Mt. Apo and other mountains on occasion. So, I prayed, "Lord, are you willing to work here so I can join you, even if it's not yet been built?" He said "Yes" and I had no idea just how incredibly successful this new ministry would become.

18.

If You Build It

The idea to build a ropes course in the Philippines wasn't new for me. I first thought about it when we lived in Manila and at various times I'd pull the idea out of my back pocket and show Krys that the vision was still alive, letting her know I was just waiting for the right season to move forward. We finally agreed the timing seemed to be right for us to prayerfully pursue this vision with the intention of finding someone to take over as the director after we built it. Krys in particular had stressed some concerns that a new ministry would take too much of my time and attention because the demands of the clinic were growing and she needed my help with the administrative needs. In addition, our organization was also growing considerably. I agreed and assured her that we could manage overseeing two completely separate ministries.

I'd watched other missionaries struggle with trying to secure sufficient funding for their projects and determined that two central things needed to happen, which were important to me personally. First, the nationals needed to take ownership and play an important role with the new ministry. Second, it needed to be domestically sustainable and not dependent on U.S. funding.

Based on my observations, and comments I'd heard from both national and foreign ministry leaders, it seemed that local Christian businessmen were not as involved as they could or should be regarding financial support of various ministry projects. In fairness, I believe their reason for holding back was due to a legitimate lack of trust that the beneficiary church or para-church organization would wisely use the money entrusted to them. Appropriate financial stewardship and accountability on the level that a successful businessman making a donation would expect was quietly questioned. Furthermore, I think it was the lack of business acumen and experience in overseeing the business side of ministry that caused trepidation on the part of business people to financially get behind what seemed to be promising ministry projects. I'd prayed about this particular issue many times as I remained firmly convinced that sustainability needed to be provided for in-country aside from some donated start-up funds from the U.S. in order to get the program off the ground, otherwise I wasn't going to pursue it.

* * *

Initially, I assumed people would be excited about a new and innovative idea to reach youth for Christ once I began sharing what I had in mind, but it didn't take long to learn that a visionary idea is hard to transfer. I knew that I needed the business community to help in order for this to work, and I was hoping that a businessman might be willing to donate some land that he wasn't using. One of my first forays in speaking with some businessmen happened when I was invited to share my vision at a local Rotary Club luncheon. Disappointment would be an understatement. I quickly realized that I was hampered by a lack of personal affiliations within the web of relational networks of people who were well connected at the higher social levels. My entire time in the city up to that point was immersion at the lower social levels amongst the poor who were our primary target group at the clinic.

I continued to take every opportunity to talk with anyone who would listen, but I remained discouraged. I had a clear idea concerning the ropes course and how it needed to be built based on my research. And most importantly, I knew without a doubt that it was going to impact youth and be a fruitful ministry. People appreciated my passion, but it seemed they just couldn't make the connection I was hoping for.

Warren Bennis said, "Leadership is the capacity to translate vision into reality." My capacity to translate even a simple idea into reality kept coming up empty. I ended up going with an alternative quotation when I realized that any vision-realization was going to be influenced more by the "If-you-build-it-they-will-come" approach as inspired by the movie *Field of Dreams*.

I finally surrendered the whole vision-casting approach and determined I would build the course on my own then let it speak for itself. I started looking for property, estimating we would need an area at least 1 hectare in size, so we looked for vacant lots situated along the outskirts of the urban growth boundary. We found a few lots that had enough potential to suit our needs, although they weren't necessarily ideal. We tracked down the owners, explained what we had in mind, then I asked if we could borrow their land for an indefinite period of time. I chuckle now, looking back at how we approached those land owners, because we naively believed someone was going to let us use their land free of charge. I kept getting dismissed with culturally respectful answers wrapped in innuendo that meant "I don't think so." I knew in my heart that God had given me the green light to move forward on this after so many years of praying, but with each disguised rejection I became more and more discouraged.

*   *   *

I've always been intrigued with the scripture recorded in Isaiah 1:18; "Come now, and let us reason together, says the Lord." A few times during my life as a missionary I have sat down and reasoned with God. Although the entire passage refers to sin, I believe God often speaks to us beyond the actual context of the story. I think the open invitation to reason with God provides a sense of wonder because of what it means—like being invited to meet an influential, well-positioned person in the community you would otherwise never have access to. He is honestly interested to hear your story or idea, and during the conversation you feel he sincerely desires to help and has the ability to do so with a genuine interest that transcends any hidden agendas or expectations.

Too often we tend come to God with a list of things we want or need. Sometimes we become so preoccupied with our own agendas that we get in a rut, which becomes the place from which we pray, and often times it's hard to see or discern the purpose of God in our lives beyond the ruts. Many years ago, I read something Chuck Swindoll wrote which made an impression that has stuck with me; "Always check your motive." I had spent eight years praying about using an adventure-based challenge course on the mission field to reach youth for Christ, and my motive had been carefully considered and incubated for a lengthy season of time.

Bob Stamps composed the song *God and Man at Table Are Sat Down*, which we often sang during chapel services in college. The title of that song became my framework as I pictured myself sitting down at a table reasoning with the Lord for the sake of the youth I wanted to help. And, He answered. A few days after the most recent rejection a friend told me that he'd mentioned my idea to a businessman who owned some land on the outskirts of town, and was willing to meet me. I didn't know this man personally, but I knew of his name because his family owns a chain of malls in the southern Philippines.

After months of searching for land this was the only positive lead we'd had, and while I was driving to meet him at the property I sensed an inner conviction from the Holy Spirit advising me not to attempt to convince this gentleman to agree with my idea—like a used car salesman trying to close the deal—as I had been doing with every other land owner I'd met thus far. God was encouraging me to stand down and let Him take care of it.

* * *

When I arrived at the site I saw the property was situated in a bowl-shaped canyon with 100' high walls on the back side and a narrow creek cutting its way down through large scattered boulders and thick vine-covered jungle. It was perfect in every way; beautiful, scenic and peaceful like a private nature reserve, covering 17 hectares (about 40 acres) with a sizable fresh water lake at the lower end that was full of Tilapia fish, which the nearby residents living along the rim would at times hike down and catch for their dinner. On the north side of the lake was a level area large enough for the ropes course facility.

The owner was waiting for us at the scheduled time, and during some cordial introductions and brief small talk I found him to be a pleasant man. He'd been somewhat briefed by our mutual friend regarding my idea to set up a ropes course and he asked for more information. I explained that I was a missionary and wanted to build an adventure-based challenge program to impact youth in the city. I was careful to hold back as the Lord had instructed me because I've been guilty of using the strength of my personality in the past to convince people by persuasion to do what I wanted, even when my intentions and motives were sincere. I didn't let my enthusiasm run ahead of me and I purposefully kept my presentation relatively low key. After so many disappointing rejections by other land owners, I was at a place, after more cultivated prayer, where I wanted to let the Lord make it happen rather than myself.

I'd learned a hard lesson a few years previous to this when I started a video-based bible school that was accredited through a U.S. bible college. Krys felt it wasn't the right ministry for us and advised that we not pursue it, but I disagreed and spent $1,000 to buy a large TV, teaching videos and the accompanying textbooks. I worked hard to get it established and did everything in my power to make it happen. I printed glossy brochures, introduced it at the city wide pastoral fellowship, and promoted it on the Christian radio station. It was a flop. It didn't work as I'd convinced myself it would because, as it turned out, people were afraid to travel to the proposed venue site in Agdao after sunset.

That experience taught me a valuable lesson about the subtle trap of trying to make things happen, which in truth is based on pride more than anything else. Not trying to close this guy, as I had been trained to do in my previous experience in retail sales, was a step of faith for me because I needed to abandon my methods—my sales pitch. I wanted to obey God and see if He would truly come through in His way.

My entire presentation took about five minutes and covered all the general project proponents. As expected, he didn't understand what a ropes course was even after I explained it, but that seemed OK. When he asked why I wanted to build the course I explained that I planned to use it to help troubled youth. He then asked how much we planned to invest and I confided that we had $5,000. After a few more questions, which I seemed to satisfy with my explanations, he said, "OK, you can use my property." I certainly wasn't expecting an immediate reply and assumed he would probably get back to us through our mutual friend, which is the preferred cultural avenue, since a third party had brought us together.

Then I said something I figured might kill the deal. I confided that I didn't have money to buy or lease the property and I wouldn't be able to do so in the future. Businessmen are smart and rarely do they allow an asset to be placed into service without some financial gain indicated on their profit and loss statement. At the very least they want to make sure their real estate tax obligation is covered which he could have rightfully asked of me since the tax wasn't a prohibitive sum. He said, "No problem. You can use it rent free for as long as you need." I was thrilled and thanked him for his gracious offer.

* * *

I wasn't aware of it at the time, but the land owner was a Christian and he later confided that he bought the property at a distressed price which he planned to develop. However, a feasibility study indicated that any development would be cost-prohibitive, for various reasons. Apparently, he had decided to dedicate the land to the Lord a few months prior to meeting me and he felt impressed to honor his promise by letting me use the property—primarily because I was a missionary who wanted to help youth.

With property secured I determined we needed to set up a non-profit foundation and apply for a business license as required by city ordinance, which would enable us to operate the ministry legally. During a follow-up visit with the land owner I asked if he would be willing to serve on the new board of directors, which I felt was entirely appropriate since it was his land. He accepted and recruited other Christian business owners he knew to join the board. We wrote by-laws and held several meetings where we began planning how the new ministry would function. I was voted to serve as the foundation's president because the board of directors felt the position should go to the person who spearheaded the new ministry idea.

We had a difficult time choosing a new name for the organization and we initially thought *Extreme Challenge* or *Extreme Adventure* might be appealing, but the word "Extreme" had become ubiquitous at the time. After much discussion, we chose *Outland Adventure* which was unique and seemed a bit intriguing. Everything was set up under the covering of our new legal entity, *Project Challenge Foundation Incorporated*, which we registered with the national Securities and Exchange Commission.

Everything was going great and enthusiasm was building with the board members once they understood the vision and independently grasped the potential of this new ministry project. Then, suddenly, everything seemed to lose its momentum because we couldn't figure out how to build the obstacles. Although the property was covered with trees, many of which were draped with hanging vines, the wood was too soft and lacked the structural integrity to support the cables required to suspend the high obstacles. So, we determined to build the course using wooden utility poles, which is what most ropes courses in the U.S. use for their structural support. There was no shortage of utility poles in the city because the local power company used them for the distribution of electricity and communications cable. Much to our delight, we heard the power company was pulling up wood poles out of the ground and replacing them with concrete poles and storing them at a yard north of town.

Initially I thought the power company was owned by the city municipality. As it turned out Davao Light & Power Co. (DLPC), which distributed and managed electricity for a large portion of the island's 20 million people, was privately owned by the Aboitiz family—a mestizo family descended from the Spanish Basques who immigrated to the Philippines a century after the end of Spanish colonial rule. This particular family oversees the country's second largest conglomerate with a personal net worth of almost $6 billion—making them the third wealthiest family in the country, according to Forbes magazine.

I'd heard it said that most of the country's wealth and influence, aside from elite political families, was controlled by about 10 families. The Aboitiz was one of those families and their group of companies included seven regional electrical power utilities, banks, food companies, real estate, construction companies, heavy industries and resorts. In all, this family managed 47 companies with an estimated worth of several billion dollars. And they alone controlled all the utility poles in the city.

We started making inquiries about the poles and how to acquire some.

We visited DLPC's storage yard and our eyes lit up when we saw huge piles of new and used wood poles neatly stacked according to their respective sizes. Some of the poles were impressive imported Oregon Douglas Firs—up to 100 feet long—used to support the main transmission lines coming in from the hydro plants up in the mountains. As it turned out, those giants would never be used because a decision had recently been made to use galvanized steel transmission towers which had a longer life span.

Apparently, as we learned, the surplus wood utility poles were a prized commodity among wealthy families who were buying them to build log homes at newly developed housing sites located at the base of the local mountain. We were advised the only way to get our hands on any wood poles would require the personal signature of DLPC's executive president, Al Aboitiz, who flew to Davao every two weeks from his home in a northern city. We were told our chances of meeting him was remote, and only people he personally knew were given permission to buy the wood poles. My heart sank, so I prayed.

A few weeks later, I was told that a meeting had been arranged for me to meet Mr. Aboitiz, but how that came to be was never explained to me. I was only told that a meeting had been set up and I was to call DLPC's office for more information.

* * *

I've known people who were rich, but I'd never known or met people who were incredibly wealthy who oversaw several companies with thousands of employees. Mr. Aboitiz's office at DLPC's corporate headquarters was expansive with wood inlaid parquet floors, expensive hand-carved wood furniture and walls paneled in rich Narra wood, also known as Philippine Mahogany. Most of the business offices I'd visited in town looked the same with white painted concrete walls furnished with cheap imported Chinese furniture.

A company secretary motioned for me and two people whom I asked to accompany me to take our seats, then after a few moments the entire wall to our left automatically opened to reveal an adjacent room where a group of men were sitting around a large conference table. One of them stood up, and starting walking toward us. He was dressed in casual European business attire and wore a thick prominent gold chain around his neck and a gold bracelet around his wrist. His hair was jet black, slightly curled, combed straight back and glistened as he walked toward us underneath the overhead lights. He shook our hands and introduced himself as Al Aboitiz.

Mr. Aboitiz exuded a professional executive presence and I was quite intimidated by his entire demeanor. He was confident but very cordial, and in a respectful manner he asked us to sit down as he walked around and took his seat on the other side of a large desk sitting in the center of the room. Small talk was pointless because he said that he only had a few minutes because the accountants, from whom he'd just excused himself, were waiting on the other side of the wall that had just closed shut giving us some privacy.

Any thought I had prior to the meeting by which I could either impress this man or convince him that my idea was worthwhile, was immediately dissolved in a single sentence that came from someone who did not mince words. Mr. Aboitiz leaned across his desk and asked, "So what do you want?" It was not disrespectful by any means, but it was pointed and concise, and like a knife it cut through all the illusions and predispositions I held prior to the meeting. The best way to describe the encounter is to provide the exact dialog.

I said, "I'm interested in starting a new program to teach Values Formation to youth." (Values Formation is a well-known term recognized by secular businessmen which actually implies the use of Christian-based values taught to employees. A phrase I knew he would understand.)

"OK, what do you have in mind?" he asked.

"We want to build an adventure-based program to challenge youth."

"OK. What type of program?"

"Well, I've talked to so many people trying to explain what it is, and no one seems to understand it." I answered.

At this point in the conversation I was so befuddled and intimidated that I actually repeated myself. Then I told him that I didn't think he would understand. In hindsight I was such an idiot. Here I was in the office with the only guy who could hopefully help me, and I was telling him that he wasn't going to understand.

"Well, I can't help you if you don't tell me what it is you want to do." he replied.

"Actually, I would like to buy some of the wood utility poles your company has stored out in the Ma-a yard, and we were advised that we need permission from you."

"Why do you need the poles?" he asked.

"I have an idea to build a ropes course and we need poles to attach the cables for the high elements."

"Oh, I know what a ropes course is."

"Sir, I've talked to so many people during the past year trying to explain what a ropes course is and they just can't grasp what I'm talking about. You're the only person I've met who knows what a ropes course is. May I ask how you know what it is?"

"I've been on a ropes course," was his surprising response.

"There are no ropes courses here in the Philippines that I'm aware of. Where did you see a ropes course?"

"Every year we take teams of engineers to the States for training with various utility companies so we can learn about new technology. I've been to several states and two years ago, while we were in Atlanta, Georgia, the utility company we partnered with took us to a ropes course facility for team building."

"How was it? What did you think?" I asked.

At this point heaven opened up and shined down into the room. That man's entire demeanor changed, and his eyes lit up as he spoke from his heart. He looked at me and said with every word carefully chosen, "It was a life-impacting experience!"

19.

Outland

For the next 45 minutes, Mr. Aboitiz, who by that time insisted we call him "Al," forgot about the accountants waiting in the adjacent room with their spreadsheets and gave us his undivided attention. I responded to his previous comment by saying that we wanted to provide the same life-impacting opportunity for youth to experience, exactly as he had on the ropes course in Atlanta. I shared with him stories about hopeless teenagers in Agdao trapped in lifestyles that were breeding grounds for drugs, violence and delinquent behavior, whereby they were becoming more marginalized, all of which was being reported in the local papers with some of the youth landing on the DDS hit list.

Mr. Aboitiz embraced the idea because he identified with the potential it held. Furthermore, he realized I had presented an opportunity for him to take a measure of ownership in order to improve on my idea and ensure its success, which I had not expected going into the meeting. What happened next helped me learn something very important in ministry. Sometimes we don't have the resources, connections, or even the influence necessary to see something succeed, regardless of how good the concept might be. Ministry leaders may conceptualize a ministry idea while business leaders bring resources, funding, and their relational network to help it become a reality. Sometimes a business leader can also expand the initial vision or conceptualization, and that's exactly what happened when Mr. Aboitiz suggested we take the vision to a higher level in order to help ensure its success. I was not prepared for what came next.

Mr. Aboitiz explained that the Aboitiz Foundation, which is governed by various Aboitiz family members, is supported by annual donations made by each company within their portfolio. Since education is valued by the family, a significant amount of money is earmarked to construct classroom extensions for public schools in the region covered by DLPC's power grid. In addition, each family member is given discretionary oversight to advocate for the funding of a "pet project."

I wasn't entirely sure why he was sharing all this until he tied it together. Mr. Aboitiz realized a ropes course targeting youth could actually help his foundation have a deeper impact on education beyond the funding of new classrooms. I walked into his office with an idea which he used to propose a much more expansive vision. The particulars and details were worked out later, but in a nutshell Mr. Aboitiz committed that his family's foundation would fund the construction of the entire facility (including two open air native-style dormitories). He also encouraged us to developed a specialized 3-day youth program for high school students and said the Aboitiz Foundation would provide all funding necessary to run the programs. The operational budgets for those programs, which were later referred to as "camps," included the costs for all meals, training materials, souvenirs such as T-shirts, and Bandanas for the students to take home, funds to cover staff wages, and unlimited free use of electricity. He told me that DLPC's public relations office would liaison with the regional Department of Education to make sure that students would be allowed to participate in the programs. Furthermore, we were advised that his staff would write the proposals for funding requests to the foundation on our behalf, which Mr. Aboitiz would personally sign and advocate for, ensuring that the funds were released.

I realized God was using this man as a catalyst to help bring the vision together as a viable and sustainable ministry endeavor. I did, however, respond by respectfully telling him it wasn't necessary to pay us to run the programs, especially in light of the fact he just offered to build the entire course for free. But he was confident in emphasizing that we needed to be financially healthy, and without the supportive funds from his foundation Outland couldn't be sustainable. I explained we'd actually planned to host private companies and charge high fees for specialized team building programs, which I hoped would meet Outland's general operating budget. He concurred and understood the need for us to market our services to private businesses, but he asked if we would prioritize the high school kids.

I explained our intent wasn't merely to run kids through a ropes course so they'd have fun—like going to the beach for a day. Rather, our objective was to teach Christian-based values and morals. Knowing such a thing would never been permitted in the U.S. I asked if the schools would be open to the idea. He assured me it would be no problem because the schools were indebted to the foundation for constructing so many classrooms throughout the region. I wasn't aware of it at the time, but I learned afterward that 83 high schools are located in the geographical area that DLPC serves. Batches of students from every one of those schools were going to be sent to participate in a 3-day program we were being asked to develop from scratch.

* * *

Mike is a guy I recruited from the States to help me build and direct the new ropes course. The previous year he had brought a small group of college students to Davao from the University of Oregon who were members of UO's Campus Crusade for Christ where Mike served on staff. "Recruited" may not be the correct word to use because several months after Mike returned to the states, he asked if I'd be open to the idea of his family moving to Davao and joining our team as full-time missionaries. He knew I was interested to start a ropes course as a ministry outreach and said that he'd love to play a part in helping me get it going. He was the answer to Krys' concern that I find someone to take the lead role and oversee the new ministry. I knew Mike was entirely capable of serving in that capacity and we were honored to receive his family several months later as our newest team members.

Mike had actually accompanied me to the initial meeting with Mr. Aboitiz, and afterward we began working on the site plans for the facility and finalized which high elements we wanted to integrate. Then we took our rough sketches to DLPC's engineering department at Mr. Aboitiz's request in order for them to make sure additional guy wires were included in the final drawings to help minimize pole movement while people were belayed from the cables.

It took about two weeks for the engineers to complete their detailed drawings, which were then sent to the finance office for budget analysis, and forwarded to management for final approval before the work order was released to the field contractors. I remember how delighted I felt after so many years of praying for this vision to come to fruition as I watched the big crane augur trucks and crews arrive at the site to begin installing the poles and connecting cables. It took about two weeks to set the poles and rig the cables to suspend large interlocked truck tires and wood platforms that were used for the high challenges. The crews were very patient with us when we requested some modifications and always said "Yes" to each request. They laughed when we commented how agreeable they were and replied that they'd been instructed to do whatever we asked because it was a personal pet project of Mr. Aboitiz.

As they were wrapping up their work, the lead crew supervisor approached Mike and I to inquire why a zip line hadn't been included in our plans. We explained that neither of us were familiar with zip lines and we didn't know how to install one, but he told us that he knew how to rig it. We had a hard time accepting that because we'd not heard of any operational zip lines in the country. He got a sheepish look on his face and said, "I'm originally from the province (*bukid*) and I built zip lines in the mountains when I was involved in illegal logging. We used them to get the logs down off the mountains and loaded onto the trucks for transport to the middlemen buyers." We had a good laugh and he continued, "We'd really like to set up a zip line for you using the extra cable that was designated for this job."

For the next few hours Mike and I watched them rig a zip line across the creek that fed the large lake. It was a relatively short zip line that was only about 50 meters long, but it provided a quick thrill ride. A second 100-meter-long zip line, suspended about 20 feet above the lake, was rigged the following year.

* * *

We were obviously overwhelmed with Mr. Aboitiz's offer to fund the construction of the facility, but it was up to us to purchase the safety equipment sourced from the States. Safety harnesses and the supportive equipment used to protect participants while suspended from the high elements or zip lines needed to have UIAA certification labels and meet specific safety standards published by ACCT (Association of Challenge Course Technology). Safety equipment is very expensive, especially when you need enough sets to run a ropes course. Thankfully we had a pair of angel investors.

Vance and Stacey Rogers are close personal friends who had financially supported our ministry for many years and committed to providing a sizable donation as seed money to help get Outland Adventure started. Of all the people with whom I'd shared my vision to build a challenge course, Vance and Stacey were the only people in the U.S. who really understood at a deep level the potential a ropes course program held as an evangelistic tool to reach youth on the mission field. From the initial conception, which I casually mentioned while visiting them during a furlough, until it became a reality many years later, they had remained fully supportive of the idea. I deeply appreciated their belief in the idea and their encouragement more than they probably realized. They had built a successful home business with an expansive nationwide network and were significant supporters of overseas missions. They believed in investing in various ministry projects around the world, whether it was orphanages, building programs, or funding new dialect translation soundtracks for *The Jesus Movie* to be shown in unreached areas. We used the seed money from Vance and Stacey to purchase the safety equipment from the States, which included harnesses, helmets, carabiners, static and dynamic climbing rope, Gri-Gri ascenders, lanyards, pulleys, and various resource materials published by the ropes course industry that was used to train people how to facilitate programs.

In the meantime, while we were waiting for the equipment to be shipped from the U.S., Mike and I began planning the 3-day *Great Adventure Camps*, which is the name we decided to call the programs. We spent a lot of time discussing how we would integrate the gospel message into the camps. Interestingly, it was a secular program based in Idaho and a 25-year-old guy with greasy hair dressed in a combination of REI hiking apparel and 90s vintage grunge clothing that help solidify my belief in ropes courses.

Two years before Outland began to take shape, I had the opportunity to observe a ropes course program at a private boarding school in Northern Idaho where wealthy families sent their at-risk teenage kids. The ropes course tied in with the school's *Ascent Wilderness Program*—an outdoor-based therapeutic system focusing on trust and respect issues that were integrated into the school's overall curriculum.

Krys' stepfather, Bill, who worked in the school's maintenance department was able to get permission for me to watch a program as an observer, with the condition that I was strictly prohibited from taking any photographs due to confidentiality concerns in order to protect the privacy of the kids, some of whom were from prominent well-known wealthy and famous families.

The ropes course was built on an impressive 50' tall Alpine Tower—a self-supporting log structure, using a top-rope (dynamic) belay system. A handful of teenagers were working their way up through various vertically suspended obstacles while secured to lifelines held by trained staff standing on the ground. I was intrigued as the lead staff facilitator patiently encouraged one particular kid, who happened to be significantly overweight, while he belayed him. When the kid reached the top of the tower and stood on a cross beam about 40' off the ground, the facilitator asked if he'd be willing to rappel down while a belayer on the ground held his safety line. He seemed comfortable with the idea until the facilitator motioned for the smallest kid in the group to stand in as the newly designated belayer using a Gri-Gri assisted braking belay device. The facilitator was entirely confident the rigging would hold because he positioned himself as a tied-in backup belayer, and he'd also set up a separate master point anchor that served as a redundant backup.

The fat kid at the top of the tower was convinced the smaller kid on the ground was going to accidentally lose control and let him fall to his death because the physics didn't compute. The senior facilitator had effectively set up a "trust event" whereby the larger kid needed to overcome his fear and trust that the smaller kid could bring him down safely. Ropes course facilitators use a philosophy known as "Challenge by Choice." Participants are never coerced, manipulated, or forced to participate, nor are they mocked or ridiculed if they choose not to join. Instead, they're encouraged but given enough time to process, and hopefully overcome their fears.

After 20 minutes, and a lot of positive encouragement from the facilitator, that fat kid let go of his death grip on the log and released himself from the tower. The smaller kid slowly lowered him to the ground where they immediately hugged each other. It seemed rather insignificant watching that as an observer, but it was clearly obvious the fat kid had been profoundly impacted by the experience. He actually started crying when he finally touched the ground and realized he was safe. Then the facilitator patiently debriefed those kids by asking them to share how they felt before and after the challenge. He also encouraged the larger kid to talk about trust issues in his own personal life and how he might be able to relate what he'd just experienced to overcoming life's challenges. I was very impressed.

I introduced myself to the lead facilitator during a break and explained that I was a missionary serving in Asia and was considering building a ropes course to help reach disadvantaged youth offenders living in poverty. I asked for his personal opinion and any advice he could provide. He said, "The kids enrolled here are rebellious kids whose parents don't know what to do with them. We have a good academic program with great teachers and counselors who do everything they can to help the students. Over the years we've witnessed that it's their experience in the *Ascent Wilderness Program* and here on the ropes course that finally gets through to them. It's unquestionably the most effective part of the entire program."

Watching the demonstration and hearing that facilitator affirm the effectiveness of the ropes course was very convincing. I knew if a secular organization was seeing tangible results then it also held the potential to be just as impacting if we used those same challenges to share the gospel with young people.

Mike understood that Outland wasn't conceptualized to be just another program masquerading as a watered-down Christian witness. He drew from his ten years of experience working on staff with Campus Crusade, and I really give him credit for developing the *Great Adventure Camps*. He did an excellent job putting everything together. I wanted to be intentional in making sure the gospel message remained at the forefront and was presented in a manner that youth would be able to see its relevance in their lives. Gospel sharing didn't happen during every moment nor was it presented with every challenge, but its message was carefully woven into debriefing times. In addition, being a relationally oriented person, Mike had successfully recruited and trained a small group of Filipino people who served as volunteers and helped staff the camps.

After months of planning we were ready to host our first *Great Adventure Camp*. I was excited because I knew the camps would get the attention of these kids, but I had no idea just how incredibly successful Outland would become.

20.

A Vision Fulfilled

In the early 1960s, Don Richardson and Bruce Olson independently targeted groups of people living in remote and isolated jungle areas who didn't possess anything that was considered as modern.

In the late 1990s our target group was comprised of civilized teenagers who attended government-funded public high schools. They lived in houses, had clothes, wore shoes on their feet, rode in Jeepneys, went to the malls, watched American movies, and ate food bought from the local market. Most had cheap cell phones, and they usually had a bit of pocket change to buy snacks.

Richardson and Olson were looking for redemptive analogies embedded in the uncivilized Sawi and Motilone cultures in order to help primitive people see a remnant of God's witness within their cultural beliefs.

As a missionary I was searching for a way to reach youth who, unlike the Sawi and Motilones, had an understanding of God and didn't require contextualizing a biblical meaning, and weren't subjected to animistic rituals requiring them to thrust their fist into a rotting human corpse as Richardson described, or endure demonic power encounters facilitated by witch doctors. My plan was to bring them to a place, even if only for a moment, which would enable them to experience God during a "moment" of vulnerability.

The challenge course enabled us to use various analogies to demonstrate the meaning of the gospel message in ways that were relevant to a teenager, particularly regarding fear and insecurity. For example, the safety equipment helped cultivate their trust in God as they learned to trust the harnesses and lifelines while suspended from cables high above the ground. We used that trust, coupled with their vulnerability, to serve as a bridge to bring youth to Christ on a personal level. Unlike anything they'd experienced directly with

God prior to coming to the camps, they began to understand His grace was sufficient to overcome what they feared most—the complexities and the chaos that life threw at them as teenagers.

* * *

The concept of using a ropes course to reach teenagers with the gospel message was incredibly simple, yet profoundly effective and fruitful. We helped students step experientially into a spiritual transformation, and they were responding to the gospel message at a level beyond what I anticipated. I believe much of our success was due to the facilitators who, over time, became more effective in their ability to share the gospel with each new camp. I noticed the effect on the students was directly reflective of the level of vulnerability each facilitator was willing to demonstrate. Students were the most responsive when the facilitators shared their own stories and were honest in talking about sins they struggled with, hatred they'd had towards their parents, sexual abuse they'd endured, or even crimes they'd committed. One of the most profound and impacting camps we hosted occurred when a former well-known gang leader gave his life to Christ and shared his testimony with the students for several hours, after which he gave an invitation to accept Christ.

Outland's reputation was growing and people began seeing the results with the students were both measurable and transferable not only back in the schools, but also in their homes. Principals were commenting about the dramatic changes they were seeing in the attitudes of students who previously were troublemakers in the schools. Parents were writing letters, sharing how Outland had changed their son or daughter to the extent they were apologizing and repenting to their parents about their rebellion. Many students kept confiding to the facilitators how much they hated their parents, then returned home crying and asking for their forgiveness.

We received a handwritten letter from Weng Pelobello, a Christian school counselor who shared a story about one of the students from her school who attended one of the camps. She wrote, "The first day of school Bonie punched a gay student inside the campus. He is known to be a bugoy, maldito (a brawler). He has lots of enemies, not just in the school campus but also in their neighborhood. He loves teasing other people. When I found out there was going to be a camp, Outland Adventure Camp, I really asked the teacher who's in charge of this activity to let Bonie join and include him on the slot because I heard that OA camp focuses on spiritual awareness and values formation. I was so glad that he was included in the list of participants of the camp. Indeed, that helped him to know God. After the camp, he became a different person and always goes to church, joins prayer meetings, Bible studies and even outreaches. He loves to share his testimony of how God changed him." Unfortunately, Bonie died from Dengue Fever two months later but Mrs. Pelobello's letter continued; "Many were amazed of that sudden change in Bonie. His death made a great impact on his classmates, friends and even those who once hated him."

* * *

Two staff members and a community relations representative from DLPC always conducted preliminary visits at each school scheduled to send students in order to brief them regarding what to expect and how to prepare themselves. We usually followed up with the schools after the camp in order to make sure everything had gone OK and the students were doing well. Our Filipino staff kept encouraging me to accompany them during these post-camp visits, but I tended to decline their invitation because of my busy schedule.

"You really need to see for yourself what happens when we visit these schools," they continued to press me.

I eventually agreed to go with them to a provincial school situated in the middle of an expansive banana plantation about an hour's drive northwest of Davao. As we entered the school compound I noticed a huge yellow banner suspended from the side of a classroom building with brightly colored letters that said, "Welcome Outland Staff!" Students and teachers were gathered outside under a tree, and I could see they had prepared a meal for us, spread out on a large bamboo table. I turned to my staff sitting in the car with a puzzled look and they said, "We get the same response at every school we visit after a camp!"

As I opened the door and stepped out of my van a teacher introduced himself as he walked up to me; then he embraced me and started crying. After a few moments, he stepped back and with tears in his eyes, said, "I'm 30 years old and in all my life I've never experienced what I did at Outland when I accompanied my students as one of their chaperones. I've attended church all my life but I've never realized Jesus could impact my life the way He did at Outland. Outland changed my life. It really changed my life! Thank you so much for letting us come to your camp. I'll never be the same."

* * *

The *Great Adventure Camps* continued to be immensely fruitful and countless students were embracing Christ. Outland formerly started operating in 2001, and over the years I'd kept Mr. Aboitiz updated through the liaison people he'd designated to work directly with us. Every request I made, regardless of how big or small, was always accommodated. Seven years later, in early 2008, I requested a personal meeting with Mr. Aboitiz, whom I hadn't seen since 2001, in order to discuss my idea to expand the facility. That same personal connection I enjoyed during our initial meeting picked right up again when he welcomed me at his office. He was very friendly and amiable and seemed sincerely glad to see me again. We talked briefly about how Outland was doing then he said something that took me completely off guard.

"I know what you're doing out there at those camps with the students," he said. "You're sharing the gospel with those kids!"

His tone was a direct and I was a little bit taken aback, unsure what to say or where he was going with such a comment. I'd never fully disclosed our intention to share the gospel with the students. Instead, I was depending on the unspoken nuances common in the culture, which I'm sure he'd picked up on during our initial meeting when I was forthright in explaining that we planned to use a ropes course to share "Values Formation", which implied Christian moral and ethical teaching.

Then with a smile he said, "God knows those students need to hear the gospel! You keep doing what you're doing out there and don't let anyone try to stop you."

Mr. Aboitiz agreed with my proposal to expand the facility. Then I found myself once again listening to a proposition that was so unusual I assumed he must have been thinking about it for quite some time before we'd met.

"Matt, of all the programs that our foundation funds throughout the entire country, Outland is by far the most successful. We're very impressed with the camps and the results we're seeing as it impacts the lives of those kids. We're also receiving very positive feedback from the teachers and principals."

I replied with a courteous, "Thank you."

Then he continued. "I'd like to ask you to consider something. If you're willing to create a separate leadership development program for some of the students who participated in the camps, whom you personally recognize to have leadership abilities, our foundation is willing to fund their entire college education. Furthermore, they would be guaranteed employment with one of our companies upon graduation."

I was dumbfounded, shocked, and astounded all at the same time. I left the meeting overwhelmed at the favor God had given us with this man and how God was using him to help empower a ministry He was blessing. At no time did Mr. Aboitiz ever try to micromanage us, or attempt to control or influence the programs. He believed we were fully capable and respected that we were missionaries who weren't being paid, which may have helped win his favor. He knew we were running Outland to serve the youth of the Philippines.

The staff and I discussed how we could develop the leadership programs as Mr. Aboitiz proposed, which would be separate from our *Great Adventure Camps*. We needed time to work on it and determined to have a program ready to begin sometime after the regular camps were completed by Christmas.

A few months later while I was in the U.S. taking care of some family business I received an urgent message that Al Aboitiz had died.

* * *

Al's position in the company was filled by his younger brother, Jim, who drove to the site to meet with me after I returned from the States to affirm his commitment to Outland. We talked for quite a while, and I took the opportunity to share some thoughts I had to help expand the programs. He agreed with what I'd laid out, which included redesigning and doubling the size of the existing ropes course facility and replacing the wood poles with taller concrete poles. I also requested if he might be willing to fund the construction of larger dorms, which he agreed to do and directed me to meet with the company architect. Jim actually demonstrated quite a bit more favor towards Outland than his brother. It was later confided to me by a senior DLPC manager that it was Jim's way of honoring his brother because he knew Al really believed in Outland.

Mike had already transitioned back to the States with his family a few years prior to this time. Another American missionary initially offered to take the lead role in managing Outland, but he also moved on after a brief season when he was asked to serve as the new national director of his mission, which required him to relocate his family to Manila.

21.

Ministry and Revenue Engines

As I've previously written, the staff was growing in their ability to effectively share the gospel, and every camp provided three days for them to systematically share various truths of the gospel message as they walked the students through the program. In addition, the students felt safe to talk about their personal struggles during debriefing sessions. The Holy Spirit was drawing them to repentance at those camps.

The more time I spend living in Asia the more understanding I gain regarding the depth of shame that Asians deal with. "Guilt–Innocence" is the prevalent force in the west which we see throughout our culture and society. However, "Honor–Shame" is the predominate force in Asia. A typical gospel presentation in the U.S. would address our sin and subsequent condemnation by God. While that's biblically true, such a presentation to a person in Asia leaves out a significant aspect of the gospel relevant to their understanding, respective of shame in addition to "Guilt–Innocence." Our Filipino facilitators were able to reach the students on a cultural level by using their language and its meaning, which touched on the "Honor–Shame" forces they deal with by focusing the gospel presentation toward realigning their "losing face" or shame with God's glory — given to us in Christ.

We experienced the same thing with our patients at the maternity clinic, many of whom carry the weight of incredible shame that comes from having a baby out of wedlock or being the victim of rape. Many patients are used by older men including policemen and businessmen who manipulate and coerce a girl, who may be twenty years younger, to have sex and serve as a type of mistress. A patient is much more open and responsive to the midwife who is sharing the gospel respective of her shame and allowing the Holy Spirit to bring healing and redeem her honor than she would be if the midwife simply shared the four spiritual laws and attempted to lead her in a sinner's prayer.

Students at Outland were likewise responding to the Holy Spirit ministering to their feelings of fear and shame. During free times, students were taking the staff aside and confessing their sins and asking for prayer. Common themes of confession kept surfacing; hatred for their parents, shame from sexual acts including experimenting with homosexuality, anger, and disrespect for anyone in authority. I've never seen youth or even adults respond to Christ in the manner those students did at Outland. They were broken and wanted to restore their honor with God. We often heard students tell us they didn't want to leave after three days, so we formed an informal church that met at Outland once a month. All campers were welcome to attend and bring a friend, which many did for the next several years. We also hosted larger events at the city's performing arts auditorium where we brought in guest speakers and had times of worship.

In addition, we hosted special programs for other ministries. For example, *Compassion International* brought kids who were sponsored by Americans, and a local science and technology college sent 800 students by batches to our camps over the course of three years. One of the most extraordinary camps happened when a Filipino Christian missionary who was working undercover with Muslims in deep central Mindanao for several years using the strategy of friendship evangelism brought a group of Muslim youth for a 3-day program, which was the first time for Outland to host Muslims. He had never openly shared Christ and asked us to present the gospel to them.

During the second night, one of our newest staff members, whom we referred to as "Zap" was a Muslim youth who embraced Christ at one of our *Great Adventure Camps* earlier that year and was water baptized in Outland's lake a few months later. He agreed to share his testimony that evening, which prepared the Muslims campers for what happened the following day.

At the top of the hills surrounding Outland is a large natural cave that we often took groups to for discussion. The cave is about 100 meters long, and when the flashlights are turned off it becomes pitch black dark. We often witnessed incredibly powerful and deeply moving encounters when we took teenagers to the cave as the Holy Spirit began moving in their midst.

At some point during the sharing time inside the cave the Filipino missionary began crying and asked the Muslim teenagers to forgive him for what he was about to share. He went on to explain that he was a Christian and had been intentionally befriending them so he could tell them about Jesus, but confessed that he was scared. He proceeded to give his testimony and told them he is no longer afraid and was even prepared to die if that's what it would take to share Christ with Muslims. His testimony became the catalyst for God to move. The Islamic spiritual leader who accompanied the youth during the camp as a chaperone spoke next. He confided that his life was a lie, that he appears clean and righteous on the outside, but inside he is black and a sinner. He told the missionary that he loved him and still wanted to be his friend and confessed he wanted to accept Christ. He and twenty-four Muslims responded and accepted Christ in that cave.

Another memorable camp was the time we hosted a group of youth offenders the city was struggling to manage. There's been much discussion by governments and children's rights advocates regarding the problems of youth in conflict. Many are convinced the cause is poverty or the effect of societal problems. Poverty being the primary cause is obviously arguable because youth offenders emerge from the middle and wealthy classes in all societies. It has been my observation, especially while living in Agdao, that much of the problem seemed to stem from the lack of positive support from the parents, which entices youth to seek out the support of gang members (*barkadas*) who provide acceptance and the appearance of positive support— leading to risk taking behavior.

We contacted the Davao City Social Services and Development Office (CSSDO) with a proposal, requesting they allow us to host a group of habitual youth offenders who were in continual conflict with the law. We explained what we hoped to accomplish and offered to host the program free of charge. The CSSDO agreed and suggested they send a few police officers to be present during the camp to act as a deterrent in order to ensure the youth would behave and not try to run away. We respectfully declined that offer because any police on site would certainly compromise our ability to earn their trust.

The reason this camp impressed me so much is because those particular teens were raw. Raw in the sense they came to the camp with no pretenses. They didn't wear masks, pretending to have their lives together or try to hide their faults. Surprisingly, of all the camps we hosted during the previous years, these youth offenders were the most open during debriefs. I think our staff got more out of that camp than the participants did!

* * *

All ministries evolve over time, and I was honored to watch Outland change and develop as the years went by until I realized another truth in ministry, which actually became one of our weaknesses. It's very difficult to sustain a ministry with part-time volunteers. It worked for a few years, but to truly reach its potential, the ministry needed full-time employees who deserved to be paid fair wages. This was needed to ensure longevity that carried over from one season to the next, enabling the staff to continually draw on the personal experiences of previous camps. The Aboitiz Foundation provided a line-item wage stipend worked into the budgets they allotted for each camp. That money was given to our volunteers for each day's work as a facilitator, but there were off-seasons that lasted several months when we didn't host the *Great Adventure Camps*. Private companies were scheduling team building programs during those times and we paid the staff bonuses based on the revenue we earned from each program. However, we might go several days at a time with nothing on the calendar. Subsequently, it simply wasn't feasible for us to commit to paying the staff full-time salaries for infrequent work.

Admittedly, I assumed that if I could trust God to provide for my needs as a missionary then the staff could do the same, and I tried to retain their service as volunteers based on that mindset, which was entirely wrong, and God convicted me. At various times over the years, Krys and I put in money we'd received from donors to keep Outland afloat, but it wasn't sustainable. Subsequently we ended up losing several key facilitators who were honest in admitting that although they loved working for Outland, they needed to have consistent wages to help support their families.

It takes money to meet the legitimate needs that ministry requires as it grows in order to pay employees, fund capital expenditures, and pay for office space. In order to entertain corporate clients, we needed a professionally presentable office commensurate with the level of programs we were marketing. Our office staff realized that business clients were judging our program based on how our office looked, and we were renting a cheap drab looking office with worn out avocado-green color linoleum on the floor. Clients were walking away because we lost legitimacy in their eyes based on the office presentation. We had to relocate the office, buy new office furniture and outfit the staff in presentable uniforms. In addition, the safety equipment was very expensive and needed to be upgraded every couple of years. At one point, I think we had $20,000 invested in safety equipment alone.

It's been said that critical mass is the point at which a growing company becomes self-sustaining. Meaning, it is no longer dependent on additional outside investment to remain financially viable. During our eighth year of operation we hit critical mass, but with reverse implications. We started a slow descent in the opposite direction like a roller coaster car that slows to a stop as it reaches the apex but lacks enough momentum to get over the top, causing it to slowly move backwards down the track in the wrong direction. Critical mass for Outland was the point where we found ourselves with far less money than we needed to remain viable.

I decided to approach Jim Aboitiz again with a request I wasn't entirely sure he'd agree to. I proposed building the longest commercial zip line in the Philippines with the intent to open it to the public as a separate stand-alone attraction and charge people a fee to ride. I knew we needed an additional revenue engine or Outland was going to dry up financially, and I believed a commercial zip line would bring in enough revenue to keep us going. Surprisingly, Jim agreed and sent crews to install the new zip.

At the time, it was the tallest and longest zip line in all of Asia, and it was also the fastest. In fact, it was so fast it took us months to figure out how to safely stop our staff members who were volunteering as guinea pigs while we designed and tested the braking systems. Initially, the angle of descent was too steep, and we clocked our staff at speeds exceeding 120 kph along the run-out, which was entirely too fast! We were able to adjust the cables and install a floating brake block to help dissipate the kinetic energy before riders reached the primary braking system. Safety had always been a priority at Outland so we had a secondary cable installed along the primary zip line, which served as a back-up. Every rider would be independently harnessed into both cables in case one of the zip cables failed. After a year of testing we finally opened it to the public when we were able to lower the speed to 80 kph and were absolutely confident the riders would be safe.

We printed and distributed fliers around the city announcing the new attraction, which we had named the "Xcelerator." During the first couple of months only a few people came to ride the new zip line. Disappointment with the low turnout prompted me to hire a videographer to film and produce a 30-second TV commercial. The cameraman and a girl "model" rode the zip line with the cameraman positioned backwards about 20 feet in front of her. This allowed him to film her fear induced facial expressions and record her screams as she rode face first in a superman position down the line. We thought the commercial turned out great and we purchased spots to air during prime-time TV on the local cable channel.

Then the tsunami hit. Over 10,000 people rode the zip line that year earning Outland three million pesos of revenue—$70,000 based on the dollar-peso exchange rate at the time. We charged ₱300 per ride, which was equivalent to the national daily minimum wage. The relative value compared to a commercial zip line operating in the U.S. charging $50 per ride would be $500,000—meaning that amount of money in a third world economy was the equivalent of earning a half million dollars. Finally, we were at a place where we could afford to pay for a full-time staff, which had grown to about 24 employees.

We also earned 50% additional revenue from selling T-shirts, soft drinks and photos we were able to take of riders as they came down the line. Somehow the Coca-Cola and Pepsi heard we were opening the new zip line and they sent representatives to negotiate for exclusive beverage rights. No one else had a commercial zip line and they felt it was an opportunity to get their foot in the door and work with companies targeting the adventure industry by offering corporate sponsorships. It was humorous watching these two soft drink companies try to outbid each other. We finally chose Coca-Cola because they offered to custom build a freestanding concrete building that would serve as a multi-purpose souvenir/ticket/concessions store. The exterior was overlaid with a giant Powerade sports drink logo to promote their product. In addition, Coke donated dozens of cases of various soft drinks and juices for us sell at 100% profit and provided us with two commercial refrigerators to keep the drinks cold.

The zip line was promoted in regional magazines and the national media highlighted it as a major tourist destination in Mindanao. We took an informal survey after the first year of operation and were surprised to learn that 80% of the riders were from Manila. People were getting on airplanes and flying to Davao to ride our zip line. After a while, businessmen from other islands started coming to inquire how to build their own zip lines. Then mayors, congressmen, and governors from all over the country started calling our office, asking if we could advise them how to install a zip line to help bring tourists to their respective geographical regions.

We learned that a handful of riders had been killed on poorly built zip lines so I decided to set up an association in order to encourage zip line owners to follow published safety standards that would ensure rider safety. Unfortunately, there were unscrupulous businessmen trying to make a quick buck by throwing up a cable and using fabricated safety equipment at the expense of rider safety. We even heard that a businessman paid off the media to keep them from reporting a tragedy that had occurred on his zip line when a father and son riding tandem fell to their deaths when their fabricated harnesses failed.

I named the association AZTEC (Association of Zipline Technology) and created a website. Initially the staff thought AZTEC was going to hurt our business because we were helping our competition, but I explained it was in our best interest. If too many riders died on poorly built zip lines, then people would lose confidence and not ride any zip lines including the ones that were safe—especially ours.

* * *

In summary of our missions work and family life up to that time…

Krys and I were overseeing two ministries that were growing and bearing fruit. For almost a decade, in addition to helping thousands of impoverished patients, the clinic had served as a training site for short term interning midwifery students who were enrolled in a program run by a separate organization. Then in 2004, as a result of a God-ordained opportunity we decided to create *Newlife International School of Midwifery*, which help students qualify for an accredited Associate Degree in Midwifery leading to the status of becoming a Certified Professional Midwife (CPM). Young Christian women from the U.S., Canada and Europe who were interested in becoming missionary midwives, while learning in a cross-cultural context to prepare them for the mission field, enrolled in our school.

Josie and Jessica were growing up to be beautiful young ladies and were enjoying school and sports at Faith Academy, a K-12 school that was established to serve the local missionary families. When the girls were still quite young we would often take them to a beach resort on another island across the bay that was accessible by an outrigger boat (*banka*) where they'd spend the whole day playing in the ocean, collecting crabs in a bucket and building sand castles. We looked forward to this as a family because it was relatively inexpensive and we often spent the night in one of the single room *buhay kubos* where the kids would sleep on foam mats on the floor. Geckos chirped throughout the night while the sound of ocean waves gently slapping against the sandy beach lulled us to sleep.

Another favorite outing, which we usually did two or three times a year, was a day trip to Eden Nature Park and Resort at nearby Mt. Apo—the tallest mountain in the Philippines rising about 9,600 feet above sea level. A prominent wealthy family recognized the potential for a mountain resort and spent ten years planting more than 100,000 imported pine tree seedlings on a vacated logged-over area situated at about 3,000 feet in elevation. The area provided a beautiful, expansive view of Davao City and the entire Davao Gulf area.

The first time we visited Eden Resort we were amazed to see thousands of pine trees that reminded Krys and me of Montana and Oregon. It was bit surreal to be living in an equatorial tropical country and smell the aroma of pine trees that are more characteristic of the evergreen forests Krys and I grew up around. The resort has several cabins for overnight visitors, a swimming pool, nature trails, a fishing village and a few fun rides for children; one of which was an improvised 50-meter-long sloping cable ride that Josie and Jessica would rode for hours.

Although we were privileged to have easy access to the ocean and mountain, I think the most enjoyable times were the adventures we had while visiting the States. Krys and I have always considered it an honor to have grown up in the Pacific Northwest and we intentionally immersed our daughters in its beauty every time we were stateside. If we were home during the summer months we'd take the girls camping, and trout fishing on the Yaak and Kootenai Rivers in Montana, white water rafting trips down the South Fork of the Payette River in Idaho, visit fish hatcheries on the Columbia River and take long scenic drives. And, of course, we'd take them snow skiing if we were home during the winter months.

Josie hammered nails into some boards during her first trip to the States when we helped build a new log home for Krys' mom and stepdad after they lost their main house to a fire. A neighbor saw the smoke while they were away at their jobs and called the rural fire department, then turned off the 5,000-gallon propane tank that fed the lights and refrigerator inside. He did his best to pull and push stuff away from the flames and heat—like the cars and various things sitting near the house. When the rural fire department arrived one of the volunteer firemen turned the propane tank back on, not realizing what he was doing and inadvertently fed propane back into the fire. The heat became so intense it vaporized the ceramic toilets and everything else in the house. All that remained amongst a giant ash heap was the slag remnants of melted coins which had been placed inside a jar that Krys' sister, Jennifer, was saving for missions Sunday. We also lost everything we'd stored in the attic when we went to the mission field. Krys lost her wedding dress and all of our wedding pictures were destroyed. I lost my prized set of ski equipment and we both lost all the childhood mementos we'd collected and saved. Although our small car, which was being stored in an improvised shed near the house, had been pushed out of the way, the heat melted the taillights and blistered the paint.

During trips in later years, Jessica took a liking to snow skiing and was thrilled the first time I led her down a black diamond run at Ski Bowl on Mt. Hood. She built new friendships with students at the local middle school where they let her play basketball although she was being home schooled during our furloughs. Those furloughs provided much needed down time and we were immensely thankful for the hospitality of Krys' dad, Steve, and his wife, Sally, who have been incredibly gracious in letting us stay in their home each time we were stateside. Their hospitality is truly unsurpassed.

Krys and I were also purposeful in teaching Josie and Jessica about God. We read to them an assortment of missionary books and Christian autobiographies every morning as they ate breakfast.

We decided to place our church attendance on pause for a couple of years in order to provide some foundational teaching we didn't feel our kids were getting at the local church we were attending in Davao. I determined the quality of their Sunday school lessons were directly proportional to the chaos caused by the most out of control kid in the class, which the teachers were unable to restrain due to cultural constraints of non-confrontation. As Christian parents, it's our hope that our children would desire to pursue God and not underestimate the influence their parents had on their lives, just as Krys and I learned to appreciate the influence of our parents who weren't perfect but strived to do the best they could in teaching us about God.

Baby number 10,000 was delivered at the clinic in the summer of 2006, and our midwifery school was enjoying full student enrollment. God had also blessed the ministry financially, and in 2009 we were able to purchase a three-story concrete building which we had relocated the clinic to in 2002 after flooding in the old clinic forced us to look for a new facility.

By 2011, the clinic was 15 years old and had celebrated the delivery of baby number 17,000. Dozens of students had graduated from Newlife School and some had gone on to serve as Christian missionary midwives in other developing countries. We were also sponsoring the college education of several young Filipino ladies from the Monobo tribe where the mission organization OMF was working.

Outland had been running for 10 years and reached 100% financial sustainability while we continued to host the *Great Adventure Camps*. Due to the success of the "Xcelerator," we built a second zip line that year and named it the "Repentor," which is 1,200' long and 300' high. Our AZTEC zip line consultancy organization had taken off more than we anticipated. In addition to serving the domestic zip line industry, we had been overwhelmed with inquiries from various countries around the world which included Japan, Thailand, Indonesia, Singapore, Cambodia, China, Mexico, England, South Africa, Canada, America, UAE, and Iran believe it or not. A group of people in the U.S. began dialoging with us about setting up a satellite AZTEC office in the States because there is no official body certifying U.S. zip lines.

Between Outland and the clinic there were 51 full-time Filipino staff members on payroll—27 employees at Mercy Clinic and 24 at Outland. This didn't include a large agricultural project we started a few years previously, which employed another 47 full-time national workers out in the province. In addition, there were approximately 30 American and Canadian missionaries serving on the team, inclusive of the husbands of our married students and their children. Krys and I celebrated our 20th wedding anniversary in June of 2011 and we felt very fulfilled and blessed.

Then, in October of that year a storm hit with full force that I never saw coming.

22.

A Perfect Storm

Although Jesus is engaged in an emergent strategy to redeem the world, the Great Commission doesn't provide a detailed step-by-step plan. Rather, He allows the strategy to emerge from people who let Him convert them at their deepest place during times of incredible vulnerability when they seek to understand how their weakness fits into the larger narrative of His work to redeem the world.

There is a difference between our relationship to the Great Commission and its relationship to us—reflecting two entirely different perspectives. We need to be careful not to be preoccupied with the former because the focus can be a bit distorted. If it's about "our" relationship to the Great Commission, then we remain as the protagonist—the main character. A deep gulf tends to separate these varying perspectives if we don't understand what obedience to Christ's mandate may cost us. Where we first need to go is "within" before we can go "out" to the whole world.

During an outing to the temple after the Day of Pentecost, Peter and John are beckoned by a paralyzed man seeking a handout. Peter provided a profoundly intimate precursor to what was about to unfold when he said, "I don't have any money, but *what I have* I give to you." Peter couldn't offer the next statement without the intimacy of the first. Before we can say, "in the name of Jesus…" we first need to ask ourselves *What do I have*?

As I was about to learn as I write in the following pages; intimacy cultivated by humility is what the Great Commission needs from us before we can bear fruit at a deeper level. And my inability to fully appreciate this led to a temporary "dead end" in my personal narrative.

The martyred German pastor Dietrich Bonhoeffer said, "When Christ calls a man, he bids him come and die." It's easy to participate in the rhetoric of the Great Commission, but lack in the "dying to self" part, which is the rightful place from where the heart of our message is able to expand outwardly and bear fruit.

I decided that if I ever wrote a book I was going to be intentionally transparent. The experience I was about to walk through was by far the most difficult thing I've ever endured in my life. It's an honest account of a crisis that broke me and subsequently taught me something about a "dying to self" conversion that was much deeper than I'd ever understood, but needed to experience.

A Filipino proverb says, "A year's care, a minute's ruin." I'll edit that to say, "Ten years' care, a day's ruin." I spent ten years overseeing Outland as its founder. That sentence is nine words long and you have a general idea what it means. What it does not describe, however, is the larger context—the hours and days and weeks and months and years of all the prayer it took to birth the vision, and the hard work to see it sustained for a decade. In the course of a few hours it was all taken away from me once the domino effect began to unfold, and I simply could not understand why nor could I do anything to stop it.

There's a story about a Filipino fisherman who sped his small motorized *banka* with bamboo outriggers to the open sea where he used dynamite to catch fish—otherwise known as blast fishing. At the end of each day he arrived back at the pier with his boat literally full after easily collecting the stunned fish from the surface where they were floating.

All other fishermen returned to the pier each day with only what they were able to catch using single lines and bait. After several days, they decided to report the other guy to the local authorities, so early one morning a policeman showed up at the pier.

The officer approached the man whom the others had accused of blast fishing and said, "We've received a report that you're using dynamite to catch fish. Is that true?"

"Well, why don't you come with me today and see for yourself," replied the fisherman.

The officer accepted his invitation, stepped into the boat and off they went. When the fisherman approached an area that looked promising he stopped the boat and tossed a buoy marking his spot, then reached into a small backpack hidden behind his seat. The officer seated at the bow was surprised to see him pull out a stick of dynamite and light it. He yelled at the fisherman, "Hey! That's illegal. You can't do that!"

The fisherman waited for the fuse to get dangerously low then tossed it in the lap of the policeman and yelled, "Join me or die!"

There are at least three sermon illustrations in that story, but I've told it to emphasize an important point; sometimes things get thrown into our laps that happen so suddenly and are so explosive in nature that we're incapable of managing it.

Betrayal is like that.

* * *

I previously mentioned Malcolm Gladwell's "10,000-Hour Rule", which is the time and experience it takes to prepare someone to reach proficiency. No amount of experience prepares us for betrayal. Its aftermath leaves us stunned, similar to being caught in the concussion of an actual explosion and the force of the shock wave leaves us vulnerable, afraid, broken, and embarrassed, but we're not aware of what we have done to justify it and grasp for reasons to understand. We desperately search for something that will provide an anchor whereby we can discern a reference point to counter what is happening, but we come up painfully empty.

It's incredibly disorienting to be betrayed by people in whom you placed a sizable trust because the experience is something your mind simply cannot process. If it's a marriage there's a level of trust in the partner to be faithful. If it's a business or ministry the leader tries to foster a culture of trust that encourages employees to take ownership in their work whereby the organization can grow. But anytime we demonstrate a degree of trust in people we expose ourselves to the chance of being disappointed and betrayed.

We were about eight years into running Outland when I named a young Filipino couple to serve as the executive directors. I wanted to recruit from within after the previous two directors, both of whom were American missionaries, had relocated their families after separately overseeing the ministry for a cumulative total of those first eight years. I felt it was time for nationals to take a more active role in the management of the ministry and this Filipino husband and wife couple, both of whom were college graduates, had been serving at Outland for a few years and proven themselves to be faithful, trustworthy and committed to the ministry. Jesus taught us to pray that the "Lord of the Harvest would send laborers into the harvest" and I considered it an honor and privilege to have them play a crucial and integral part as they labored in the harvest of seeing so many youth come to Christ.

I spent countless hours mentoring and discipling this couple, often meeting with them several times a week. Almost every aspect of the ministry was delegated to them via provisional authority under my direct oversight, which included managing the staff, running the camps, and overseeing the office.

We were approaching the time of year when the *Great Adventure Camps* were scheduled to begin and I agreed to a request from the couple for some personal time off because they had worked hard for many months, often putting in overtime, and deserved some down time prior to the busy season that was approaching.

After their return to work I invited them to meet me for lunch at a local coffee shop because I wanted to make sure everything would be ready for the upcoming camps. I noticed they were uncharacteristically sullen and withdrawn as we sat down and ordered our food, so I engaged them in some casual small talk by asking about their vacation and how their kids were doing. They responded by telling me they were resigning effective immediately, which shocked me. We've had people resign for various reasons and attrition is always a part of running any business or ministry. This couple was quite exceptional and I knew at some point I'd end up losing them when God called them to another ministry or endeavor. Leaders just always hope that losing good people will be deferred until Jesus returns.

Advising that they were resigning was the last thing I expected to hear, and it was very straightforward considering the culture. Communication styles in the Philippines involves a lot of hemming and hawing regarding a topic of that significance, which is generally eased into by way of innuendo requiring a listener to discern what people are really saying without it being stated so direct. Or people will sheepishly hand over a letter of resignation after the lunch is finished and the parties are on their way out the door.

As difficult as it was to hear their news it was troubling as I watched their behavior turn antagonistic. Then the metaphorical first grenade hit with force when I asked why their resignation was so sudden because people always provide at least a 30-day advance notification as required by the national labor laws. I vividly remember what happened next because it is indelibly etched in my memory. They said, "We're leaving because you're a liar and you're unrighteous."

Blank.

I believe God gives Christian leaders an ability to absorb a lot of things that help deflect crisis in order to effectively manage problems. I've discovered as a mission director overseeing a group of foreign missionaries that culture shock and homesickness are the primary culprits for most personal problems experienced on the mission field, which is sometimes directed at leadership—as if the leader is causing the problem. Leaders need to be adept at reading between the lines so-to-speak and try to discern what the real problem is, although it's not being communicated on the surface.

Rarely are Filipinos so direct in their communication style to lay an accusation at someone, and I was quite taken aback by such frankness and their lack of respect. Sitting down to a meal in a public setting and being told that you're a liar and unrighteous is a bit unsettling, especially when you're being identified as the antagonist, and its coming at you with pale resolute expressions from two people you have poured your life into for several years. My mind raced as I tried to land on something, anything, I might have done to cause them to conclude I was unrighteous. Every leader makes mistakes and we're sinners, but a single principle has always guided me in the ministries God had entrusted to us; protect the integrity of the organization, which begins by walking in personal integrity.

I could sense something was certainly amiss and entirely out of place considering our history working together during the previous years so I asked if they could give me an example of what I had done that was unrighteous or how I had lied.

"Well, you're just unrighteous," they replied.

I noticed the husband's face had reddened and his expression was almost defiant as his attitude against me had now become not only an indictment but a direct challenge against me as their leader. Their negative attitude and the uncomfortable atmosphere it created unfolded so fast I struggled to understand what was happening because I'd never before witnessed such behavior from this couple, or from any other Filipino person I'd known during all the years we'd lived in the country. I struggled to contain or even deflect the growing confrontation so I did my best to remain calm. Again, I asked them to give me some particulars—what had I specifically done to them or anyone that was unrighteous? Same response; "You're just unrighteous."

I decided to set the accusation aside and inquired about the upcoming camps scheduled to start the following month. Although the staff was well trained they lacked the ability to serve in a camp management capacity and I didn't feel that anyone in particular was up to the job because the camps required a lot of oversight. So I asked, "Who can you recommend to take over the staff and facilitate the camps after you quit?"

Then time stopped still for me when they answered, "All the staff are resigning and leaving with us."

Silence.

Grenade number two just detonated.

* * *

If you've watched war movies such as *Saving Private Ryan* or *Lone Survivor* you might recall when the director muted parts of the soundtrack as a sensory affect for the audience to identify with the soldier losing his hearing after a mortar explodes nearby, stunning him. He's momentarily deaf and disoriented as he struggles to understand what happened. The director may also make the camera wobble a bit and distort the picture clarity to draw the audience in deeper and help them relate to the soldier experiencing disorientation. The initial response of a betrayal creates a similar feeling for the simple reason that you have nothing by which to gauge what's happening. There's no point of reference. You're a bit disoriented as your mind struggles to process what you're hearing. A friend of mine confided that's exactly how he felt after his wife admitted that she'd had multiple affairs.

I sat in my chair dumbfounded as I stared at a plate of food I was no longer interested in eating. I was unprepared to deal with their growing antagonism because it involved more than telling me I was "unrighteous." Their entire attitude was infused with arrogant condescension. An inferno erupted inside me while listening to this couple lay down kindling soaked with contempt directed at my leadership and indicting my integrity. I decided at that time it would be prudent to leave before I said something I'd later regret so I excused myself and walked out to my car where I sat in stunned reflection.

Once I collected myself I drove out to the ropes course facility and gathered all the staff in the gazebo. I was direct and to the point.

"I was just advised that all of you are resigning. Is that true?" I asked.

Silence.

I repeated myself, and someone quietly mumbled "Yes" without looking at me.

"Why are you resigning? Is there a problem?"

Silence.

"Did I do something to offend anyone?"

Silence.

"So, all of you are resigning and no one can tell me what the problem is?" I asked.

The only response I got was a bunch of eyes looking down at the floor in silence that seemed to be protecting a degree of shame they were hiding behind. I asked a few more questions, but received the same dismissive non-response. I then instructed them to help me gather the rider safety equipment that had been used earlier that morning and put it in the storage bodega, which they did, and after I secured the lock I collected their keys and left. Four additional staff members were in the office back in town so I headed there next.

As I walked in the door all four women who served as our front office personnel stood up, walked across the room and handed me their resignation letters in unison, as if it had been choreographed. By this time I'd had enough. It's like I was dealing with some unseen force that had taken over these people. I was in no mood to ask them any questions or even listen if they wanted to explain themselves because their actions had communicated clearly enough. I collected their keys and secured the office after they left then drove home where I attempted to explain to Krys everything that had just happened.

As it turned out, there was more to come. Before the day was over I learned the couple had also written an email to the Filipino board of directors accusing me of several strong allegations before we had met together for lunch earlier that day. That was grenade number three and it had achieved its objective. Contacting the Filipino board had been a preemptive move on their part to gain advantage and effectively undermine my leadership. They had sought to make me into something that fit their own narrative, and in doing so had completely dismantled my position in the ministry.

Like a man casting handfuls of seed while walking through a tilled field, this couple had certainly sown broadly. Within a day, I lost the hearts of everyone directly connected with Outland, and not one single person stood with me, including the Filipino board members who wouldn't reply when I repeatedly tried to contact them.

Ten years' care, a day's ruin.

* * *

I was so dazed as to what had happened that I couldn't think straight. I struggled to find clarity and tried to understand what I'd done to cause the staff to resign en masse, but I was coming up empty. I could understand if I'd done something to offend the couple or caused them to lose confidence in my leadership and resign quietly, but they chose to take everyone with them.

Everything had happened on a Friday, and during that weekend I struggled to figure out how to salvage Outland. I felt compelled and obligated to keep my hand on the plow so-to-speak and not abandon the ministry by refusing to consider it was a pointless endeavor of misguided hope. I decided to report to the office on Monday and it was quite surreal sitting alone at a desk, doing my best to answer emails from businesses inquiring about team building programs or people calling about the zip lines hours of operation. I kept telling people that Outland was temporarily closed for in-service training and we planned to be open again as soon as possible. Actually, the in-service training was limited to me as the lone standing staff member because I was training myself to run an office that had always been staffed by employees.

Over the next several days I continued to reach out to the Filipino board members seeking their assistance, but they wouldn't respond to my texts or emails or offer to help me manage the crisis. I thought that surely one of them would stop by or invite me for a cup of coffee somewhere in order to at least get my perspective on what had happened, but nothing. I felt completely abandoned as I tried to restart a ministry that had grown well beyond the ability of one person to manage.

I also tried several times to reach out to the couple to see if there was anything I might have done that offended them. I was convinced there must have been a misunderstanding and I tried to give opportunity for restoration. They promised via text messages to meet with me and asked for some time to think, but it was a diversion while they ended up fleeing to another island.

I made another attempt to reach out to the Filipino board two weeks later when I wrote a personal plea to the owner of the property who had relocated to Manila several years earlier. I sent him an email requesting to speak with him in person and advised that I would be flying to Manila the following week for Immigration purposes regarding my visa renewal. I asked if he would please meet me on a set date at a particular Starbucks located in one of the large malls, and I provided a two-hour window, assuring him that I'd be there during that time. He didn't reply, and although I went to Starbucks in hopes of seeing him, he never showed up. Before I completely lost hope in the board I decided to try one more approach. Two of the board members living in Davao attended the same church so I emailed them and respectfully asked if they would be willing to have their pastor meet with all of us so we could talk with him serving as a facilitator. No response from either. I simply could not understand what seemed to be their irrationality; that my own board members were not standing with me as the founder. At that point I wasn't asking them to fix the problem. I was merely asking them to be involved.

* * *

I read an article about a study that had been done regarding impressions planted in people's minds and how difficult it is to overcome or counter an initial impression. Regardless of whether or not the impression is true the hearer privileges the initial accusation. Dan Allender writes in his book *Leading With A Limp*; "Betrayal always brings a distortion of the truth. They twist the truth to garner more power or position while belittling his rival. Part of the helplessness experienced by the victim is the inability to repair the breach and set the record straight. Any effort to do so looks defensive; any failure to mount a defense looks weak." The initial seeds that caused me to appear guilty had burrowed in so deep I couldn't overcome it no matter how desperate I wanted to repair the breach. The couple had meticulously and subversively misled the staff and the mass resignation fully legitimized the indictment against me. Sadly, that fact alone seemed to ensure the Filipino board's intent to distance itself from me.

* * *

Regardless of what had unfolded it was personally important to me as the founder of Outland to do everything I could to try and preserve the ministry. For several days, I thought and prayed about what I should do and I decided to look to the Old Testament character, Gideon, for some inspiration. The biblical narrative tells us, prior to his introduction in Judges chapter six, that the Midianites and the Amalekites banded together in order to trample down Israel's crops. The two armies mounted their camels—they were "innumerable" according to the story—and went for a joy ride through Israel's wheat fields, kind of like delinquent teenagers four-wheeling their havoc through planted fields under the cover of darkness. Fast forwarding the storyline brings us to an angel sitting under an oak tree while Gideon is in a wine vat threshing out some wheat he'd collected after the camels trotted off.

One thing in the story that intrigues me is the choice of military tactics the two armies used against Israel. It wasn't personal and it wasn't directed at flesh and blood because the story doesn't describe a battle scene involving swords slashing or arrows flying through the air resulting in thousands of dead lying on the ground—as described in every other recorded Old Testament battle scene. Rather, the enemy simply attacked Israel's harvest and not one Hebrew was killed or wounded.

I've come to believe that we sometimes fall short of interpreting significant events presented in our lives and fail to discern the larger picture. Ephesians talks about principalities and powers that we wrestle against in spiritual battles. I can't help but wonder if we as Christian sometimes miss a tactical move on the part of our spiritual enemy who may be targeting our harvest rather than us directly.

This is exactly what I believed had happened at Outland. The ministry was unarguably fruitful as many people had witnessed, and the enemy was trying to destroy the harvest. Like Gideon I was determined to collect what little I could, thresh out the wheat and replant it. I reasoned in my heart that Outland could recover and it just needed me as the founder to rebuild it while being fully convinced the Lord was going to honor my tenacity and faith.

Unfortunately, it didn't work out the way I hoped. The longer I sat in the office as the days went by the more it became evident that I wasn't going to be able to get the train back on the tracks. I simply could not find my bearings and repeatedly found myself returning back at the exact same place, regardless of whatever direction I pursued, just like someone lost in the mountains who discovers they'd been walking in circles and finds himself at the same tree stump he passed by earlier in the day. I was very much at the mercy of the antagonists whose influence over other people continued to expand outwardly even after their initial confrontation in the coffee shop. They had effectively fractured my ability to move Outland beyond the crisis and reboot the ministry.

After 30 days of reporting to the office I was faced with the inevitable. Outland had legally been set up as a foundation and I couldn't run it as a sole proprietorship and the board wasn't speaking to me, so my hands were tied. I racked my mind trying to understand why the board would turn their back on me. I thought an act of humility might get their attention, so I sent an email message suggesting they hire an accountant to conduct an internal investigation, which was prompted by my assumption the couple may have accused me of fiduciary negligence. I was in the dark about what the accusations were so I defaulted to recommending an emergency audit, convinced it would reveal something. Again, no reply but I continued to advise them I was sitting alone in the office needing their assistance, but they simply would not engage themselves.

Finally, I had no option but to surrender so I sent an email to each of the board members tendering my resignation. Two days later I received a formal reply, and surprisingly the response came from the land owner whom I tried to meet in Manila, which confirmed he had in fact been receiving my previous communications. It was simple and brief. "We accept your resignation. Thank you for all your years of service."

* * *

Everything in my life at that time went sideways, and I felt like I lived on the dark side of the moon for the next year. Betrayal is an eight-letter word that leaves a derailed train wreck of chaos in its wake that wreaks havoc in our lives. It touches who we are in our hearts and that's where the greatest loss is suffered. In my case I lost friends. I lost the respect of the Outland employees as well as the Filipino board members, and I lost my reputation amongst many business people in the community once the accusations began circulating, which brought a significant level of personal shame. I also lost my relationship with many people at DLPC whom I interacted with over the years including Mr. Aboitiz.

What office do you go to, or what Facebook page do you create to get your reputation back? What I experienced left me vulnerable, embarrassed, and wanting to leave the mission field. Some people became prejudiced against me, including a few members of the missionary community who were eager to listen in on the *bamboo telegraph* and concluded I certainly must be guilty of something quite serious otherwise the ministry wouldn't lose its entire staff. One missionary, who I was in partnership involving a large project in the province, hand delivered a letter to the clinic stating he'd lost confidence in me and walked away from the partnership, but gave no opportunity to discuss his reasons in person as a fellow missionary or a friend.

Being a strong justice person I desperately wanted to vindicate myself. Even though I lacked clarity as to what specifically had caused the crisis or what "unrighteous" thing I'd done to cause people to abandon the ministry, I knew it was all a sham, a ruse, a smokescreen, but I was absolutely powerless to overcome it and defend myself. The couple's ploy was so effective, so elaborate, and the story they told people was so incredibly convincing that everyone who heard it believed them. One of the senior staff at Outland sent me a text a week after walking off the job, exhorting me to repent and submit to the spiritual authority of the couple, primarily the husband whom he referred to as man of God. As the crisis reached its climax and during the months that followed the Lord would not allow me to defend myself, and when I attempted to do so He severely disciplined me.

As the saying goes "water seeks its own level" and I struggled to find equilibrium in order to bring balance and peace back into my life after feeling confused and dismayed. I couldn't find perspective and my heart was racked with stress. For weeks and months my prayer life consisted of three words; "Why God? Why?" I couldn't sleep well and I lost 15 pounds. I had poured my life into building an innovative ministry and endured the challenges of sustaining it for ten years. The loss was a huge hit to my self-worth and significance as a missionary. One missionary friend confided that he would have left the mission field if something of that gravity had happened to him.

I refused to take my hand off the plow, though, and the journey on which I set myself in order to figure out what happened during the year that followed was incredibly difficult and it required me to be open minded and honest. It wasn't until about 12 months later that I began to see glimpses that a secondary strand or subplot to what I thought had been the main storyline started to emerge as God began to pull back the curtain in order to give me a different perspective.

As It turned out, the betrayal and the injustice I'd suffered wasn't the main story. It never had been.

23.

The Irenaeus Paradox

In his book *Waking The Dead*, John Eldridge bursts out of the starting gate with a little-known quotation printed on a dedicated introductory page; "The glory of God is man fully alive," ascribed to the 2nd century monk St. Irenaeus. It's an intriguing statement because it implies a paradox—God's glory is connected to our redemption. I sat on that for a while and wondered if there was a connection between what Irenaeus said about being fully alive and what Jesus said about dying; "Unless a grain of wheat falls into the earth and dies, it remains alone; but if it dies, it bears much fruit"—a paradox.

In the ensuing months after my departure from Outland, as I dragged myself through early morning devotions, I so much wanted answers to why people had maligned and abandoned me. Leaving the mission field was never an option for me as a result of what I'd endured, but I felt as if half my life had been plundered. I heard it said the saddest thing about betrayal is that it never comes from your enemies. I kept trying to understand why people I considered to be my friends and knew my character had suddenly determined I was so dangerous and evil they chose to enact widespread chaos that brought a fruitful ministry to its knees. I thought the "why" questions were essential, but they were not to be the central means to resolution.

While sorting through all that confusion a friend living in another country heard about my experience and wrote the following brief story;

"Many years ago, my parents started a mission board in another country that had grown and flourished. Sadly, they went through a very painful betrayal. One man started telling lies about them and my parents' best friends/co-workers also believed him and joined in the betrayal against my parents, which led them to resign the mission they founded, and my dad succumbed to severe depression. A few years later, the man who lied about my father made a public apology, admitting that everything he had said about my parents were lies and he had done it to have power. His wife ended up committing suicide and his kids disowned him. My parents moved on and are now overseeing a thriving cross-cultural ministry."

As much as I appreciated reading his story it didn't seem to lessen the impact I found myself slogging through. As I bobbed up and down in my ocean of disorientation, a missionary friend took the time to listen to my story and discerned what I experienced may have been in line with a season of deeper pruning. He loaned me a copy of Robert Clinton's book *The Making of a Leader* and suggested it might provide some answers. The author suggests there are patterns or phases God uses to develop a leader, specifically six stages of leadership development, which he lays out in the book. To use the analogy of someone struggling in the ocean after falling overboard, I felt as though my friend had tossed me a life-ring. As I stepped inside chapter five, Clinton proposed something I'd never considered. He wrote that God will, at times, ordain a crisis in a leader's life in order to move him on to other things.

* * *

Over the course of several months, during brief unguarded moments while I was reaching for a box of crackers at the grocery store, pumping up a flat tire on Jessica's bicycle, hitting a volleyball with Josie and at other times, God dropped subtle impressions that helped provide some clarity. It wasn't, however, the clarity I'd been seeking because another storyline started to emerge that seemed to validate what Clinton was proposing.

It turns out that I'd been prompted to refocus my life, but I chose not to pay attention. For two years Krys kept telling me that she needed my help at the clinic. We were serving so many people that it was not uncommon to walk into the clinic and find it wall-to-wall with patients. The waiting room was often packed with pregnant women holding priority numbers for prenatal exams, and as a result of the backlog, "train wrecks" were happening more often in the birth rooms, which is a term the midwives use when more than ten women are delivering in a 24-hour shift. In addition, the government was enacting so many new regulations for lying-in clinics that we had to triple the number of hired clerks just to keep up with the increasing volume of paperwork and reports mandated by the Department of Health. Krys was beside herself, trying to stay on top of everything.

I justified my lack of support by asking one of the men on the team to help with administrative duties in the office, but the job was beyond what he was capable of doing even though he did his best. Truthfully, it was beyond a position of responsibility he didn't have in the ministry, which had nothing to do with his capabilities. Rather, it was a responsibility that was mine alone to bear considering my position in the ministry because decisions, guidance and leadership needed to be included along with administrative oversight that can't and shouldn't be delegated.

With each request Krys made for help I typically responded by explaining that Outland was growing phenomenally and needed my attention. Furthermore, I felt the responsibilities I had delegated to the staff, specifically key employees whom I'd empowered with some authority, were sufficient to ensure the clinic functioned smoothly, thereby providing Krys the support she needed. I believed my reasons were entirely valid, but failed to admit they were actually excuses.

An added voice running parallel to Krys' growing sense of urgency came from Gary Jones and his wife, Lynn, who returned to the U.S. after serving faithfully on our team for several years. They remained connected with the ministry with Gary serving as a board member of our US-based mission organization. During a brief two-month summer furlough I met with Gary for a cup of coffee, and at some point during our conversation he respectfully told me that he feared I was missing the place God wanted my attention. He affirmed the ministry I was doing with Outland and the impact it was having with the youth, but Gary was intentional and spoke with a heart I recognized was gleaned from learning to discern God's voice. He told me that my legacy was the ministry of the clinic and not Outland. More importantly, he said the investment Krys and I were making as a couple needed to be directed toward the young women enrolling in the midwifery school that were being trained and equipped to serve as missionaries. Gary unknowingly affirmed what Krys had been asking of me. He told me, "The clinic and the midwifery school need your attention—all of your attention. You're focused on the wrong ministry. I'm concerned that you're missing God."

Sometime after returning to the Philippines, about three years before the crisis hit, I hosted an informal board meeting and proposed to Outland's trustees that I believed it was time to turn the ministry over to another organization. I explained that we had taken Outland as far as we could, and a new organization with fresh people and new ideas would be able to bring in a new vision while retaining the initial vision we all had. Surprisingly, the board unanimously agreed and we formerly voted to look at how that transition would happen. However, for some reason I cannot explain, other than to suggest it was most probably caused by my pride and ego, I got sidetracked and determined that as the founder I was entirely capable of instilling fresh vision. I dismissed Krys' concern and what Gary had cautioned and continued to oversee the day to day operations of Outland. Eventually, a collision needed to happen as Clinton proposed, and in retrospect I realized that a betrayal was the vehicle of conflict God used to finally get my attention.

*   *   *

In his book *Jesus Outside the Lines* Scott Sauls writes, "Jesus loves the element of surprise. He loves to meet us in places where we least expect him—in places that contradict our assumptions and sensibilities, in places where we are least likely to be looking for him." It's difficult to convey in words how shattered our world becomes in the aftermath of betrayal; and as I began sorting through my life, Jesus met me at a place I didn't want to be— a place that contradicted my Christian missionary mindset. And in that place, He chose to bring me through a conversion experience that forced me to contend with my own personal ego as I wrestled with what I had come to realize; I was an unconverted missionary. In truth, I was a Christian expat living in another country and doing good things. Yes, I was seeing fruit and God was blessing our ministry, but the fruit I was seeing was not proportionate with the depth of Christ's teaching; "...but if it dies, it bears much fruit."

*   *   *

I believe St. Irenaeus was correct. He knew that man is never fully alive until he is crushed and broken and has nothing left but to abandon himself to God; and in that crushing there is evidence of God's glory. The glory of God is man fully alive. Irenaeus' quotation could read, "The glory of God is seen in the brokenness of those who abandon themselves to Him because only in their broken state do they become fully alive and bring more glory to God." A quote by the Holocaust survivor, Victor Frankl, bears witness of this; "If there is meaning in life at all, then there must be meaning in suffering. Without suffering and death, life cannot be complete." He also wrote; "The way in which a man takes up his cross gives him ample opportunity – even under the most difficult circumstances – to add a deeper meaning to his life."

It took a crisis to realign me, and I found the betrayal I encountered actually served as a regenerative force that began to reshape me in the years following. It also helped me realize I wasn't a successful missionary respective of how I was defining it. Brokenness and suffering are not just risks we take on to follow Jesus. I've come to believe they are to some degree the means of following Him. The way in which I measured our success as missionaries for many years was misguided. We can't gauge what we've accomplished on the field to be the determination of our success as missionaries. It doesn't work that way and it took a crisis to help me understand it. The salt of my mission narrative is not so much the good things I used to write about in my newsletters, but rather the fruit I'm seeing as a result of my willingness to be humble and remain broken after experiencing something that drained me.

*   *   *

Sometimes I wonder if missionaries are called to two separate target groups; the people group he's trying to reach, and himself. The experience I went through helped me to understand on a deeper level that our success with our targeted people group is conditioned on our own personal growth. Or, perhaps better expressed; the success we have with the people we're trying to reach is directly proportional to how much we're willing to lay it down. Success or fruit is very much a direct reflection of dying to self. Understanding that was a watershed moment for me. I don't think any Christian chooses to sit on the sidelines. Rather, we give ourselves to be exposed and vulnerable and to be wrung out, only to learn after many years that we strive to be at our best during our worst, and our strength comes from our admission of weakness and a learned willingness to walk in it.

* * *

Many people have asked me to share my side of the story and explain what really happened at Outland because they're quite curious. After all, it does make for an interesting and compelling story; why would everyone in a ministry just walk away within a day and provide no reason or explanation. Actually, I believe God kept it hidden from me because it had been there under my nose the entire time. God knew if I had the information to defend myself it would have empowered me to plead my case, right a wrong and ultimately vindicate myself.

I did share my story with two or three people in an attempt to defend myself until I realized something; it didn't help or change anything. I realized that only a few people in our lives are actually 100% true to us, and sharing our stories at a deeper level doesn't necessarily change where people are in their relationship with us. I also learned that struggling to defend myself kept me from forgiving people.

Most importantly, I discovered through times of prayer that God didn't want me defend myself and He drew the metaphorical line in the sand beyond which He didn't want me to cross. I spent months wrestling over this because, as I previously wrote, I am a strong justice person; but God eventually showed me that He was going to use the experience to refine me. I was left with no options. I did not hear God speak to me audibly, but His message was abundantly clear when I sensed He would not tolerate any attempts to defend myself, and I was severely reprimanded the two times I attempted to do so.

As for the board's abandonment, I don't have an answer other than to say they were faced with an incredibly complicated problem that was practically impossible to manage or reconcile. From their perspective, it didn't matter who was right or wrong. Truth often loses its way amidst a betrayal where the sphere of influence reverberates amongst several people. The mass resignations legitimized the accusations in the eyes of everyone, regardless of whether it was a ruse or if it was legitimately justified. Furthermore, any attempt to conduct an internal investigation, which I requested, would have only exacerbated the problem and made it even more convoluted.

I could claim what happened at Outland with the mass resignations caused dishonor to the board members, respective of their personal honor within their social networks. The covering of their shame took precedence over critically examining what had happened. But I don't feel that's a righteous position from which I should speak because it tends to imply blame at their expense without making provision for them to defend their actions. From the perspective of the "Honor–Shame" cultural forces at play, the action of the board, or what I felt to be the lack thereof, was entirely understandable. In fairness to the board, I have to say truthfully that it really was an unusually complex and irreconcilable problem for them to manage. I don't necessarily agree with what they did, but I understand why. It's important to recognize the cultural forces at play and I realized later that the crisis also brought shame to them because they were forced to explain to other people, including the Aboitiz Foundation and Davao Light, what happened as they worked to protect Outland's integrity. It's also possible they may have been attempting to hide what they perceived was my apparent shame. Their choice to disengage from me might have been motivated to protect and cover any shame that may have been exposed if they would have met with me. Furthermore, they were also presented with a sensitive cross-cultural component (I'm a Westerner) by which they were restrained in dealing with the problem with me as a foreigner, and in truth they probably didn't know how to manage that.

The beauty or the brilliance of the God-ordained crisis I experienced is that He cleared the table in order to force me to surrender. It took me a long time to see this, but once I did it made sense. In one clean sweep God removed everything I needed to rebuild the ministry. If the couple had been successful in only swaying a handful of people, then I could have continued to steer the ministry. Or, for example, if the board had come forward and stood with me, then I could have re-started the ministry by my own ego, determination, tenacity and fortitude, which is exactly what I would have attempted without hesitation. God in His wisdom and mercy left me with nothing whereby I could have gotten that ministry back on its feet. He removed all the pieces in order to realign me back to the clinic, just as Krys had been asking and Gary had been exhorting.

* * *

Clinton writes that God uses various processes to provide guidance throughout the life of a leader as he or she matures and develops in their position. Two of his listed processes, the *crisis process* and the *conflict process*, as he calls them, are the most difficult to discern the working of God—and these are the two I experienced.

A friend of mine, Bill Wilkinson, is a certified counselor and registered psychotherapist who has been a career missionary for 30 years with Overseas Missionary Fellowship. Bill did his doctoral dissertation on shame—specifically shame amongst Western missionaries serving in Asia. His research measured how missionaries cope with or defend against shame based on the Compass of Shame Scale which identifies four responses; Attack Others, Attack Self, Withdraw and Avoidance. I think I cycled through each of those during any given day, and for a long time I let the betrayal define me. Admittedly, I didn't like what I saw in the mirror. But I came to learn that God was testing me and teaching me to be dependent on Him in light of the fact there would be no resolution.

As difficult as that experience was, the lessons I learned and continue to discover have proven to be extremely valuable. I think the prospect of our true success as missionaries hangs on a single thread of understanding; the need to die to self as Jesus likened by using the image of a wheat head falling to the ground, conditioned with a caution that it cannot bear fruit and will remain alone if it refuses to succumb to everything we fight to protect it from dying.

We continually petition ourselves so that we can die and lay it down, but the tranquil détente we tend to embrace is likened to a pillow that catches the wheat head and provides a soft landing—dampening the shock of hitting cold, hard dirt. And there we remain, suspended on the pillow, as it were, finding solace where we assume to thrive in our Christianity. And it seems to work. We attempt to do our best, navigating life's breakwaters during our morning quiet time only to find ourselves capitulating to the need to steer through the economy of life that opposes our well prayed intentions the previous hour, before facing the challenges life throws at us after we say "Amen."

The Apostle Paul said that he came to a place in his life where he welcomed suffering because he knew the resulting fruit would be well worth the ordeal. I am certainly far from the place Paul was, but I have a better understanding of what learning how to limp means, and in that disability we are better positioned to bear more fruit. As the Psalmist writes in Psalm 119:71 (NIV), "It was good for me to be afflicted so that I might learn your decrees."

24.

"It All Counts"

When I was fifteen years old, my dad arranged for my brother, Scott, and I to go on a four-day float trip through Hells Canyon, the deepest river gorge in North America. The gorge cuts through a pocket where the Salmon River Mountains and the Blue Mountains meet along the northeast border of Oregon and western Idaho. It's an impressive canyon carved out by the Snake River, having towering walls nearly eight thousand feet above the river at its deepest point. At various locations throughout the canyon the peaceful river suddenly turns violent, producing Class III and IV whitewater rapids.

After arriving at the launch site just below Hells Canyon Dam I took one look at the raft and realized we had entered the big leagues. Floating peacefully on the river just a few feet from the shoreline was a 30-foot-long 10,000-pound rigid inflatable raft tethered to a large rock. It was an impressive sight; a monster compared to the truck tire inner tubes we floated on when we drifted down the Powder River that flows relatively peaceful through Baker Valley. The raft was designed to carry 15 people on the open bow. The midsection was used to haul enough food and camping equipment to outfit the entire group for a week. The three-member crew included a river guide, a cook and a boatman who stood on a platform towards the rear, manning an outboard motor used to maneuver the raft as needed around obstacles and through rapids. A flex point in the middle allowed the raft to bend or fold vertically as it passed through the larger rapids.

Those four days were an incredibly thrilling adventure, especially for two young boys who had never experienced anything on that level. The height of the towering walls standing at attention along both sides in the deepest section of the canyon were impressive as was the various wildlife we were able to observe, in addition to the sheer excitement of the ride itself. Undoubtedly, though, the most exciting highlight that stood out for the entire group was day two when we experienced Granite Rapids, which according to American Whitewater (AW) is a Class IV rapid described as; "Intense and powerful requiring precise boat handling in turbulent water. It may feature large, unavoidable waves and holes or constricted passages demanding fast maneuvers under pressure. Scouting may be necessary the first time down. Risk of injury to swimmers is moderate to high, and water conditions may make self-rescue difficult."

I'm not sure if the guides were intentionally stirring up feelings of excitement amongst our group as they openly discussed concerns about those particular rapids, or if they were genuinely a bit uneasy. The validity of what we'd come to realize was in fact their anxiety was confirmed when we passed a jet boat that had flipped over as it tried to navigate upstream through Wild Sheep rapids. It was submerged upside down in the middle of the river with only a partial section of its aluminum hull visible above the water line.

About a mile down river from where that boat had flipped is a small sandy beach the boatman steered toward and parked the raft. We all disembarked and the guide advised us that Granite Rapids was just around the next bend. He asked us to sit tight for about 30 minutes while he and the boatman hiked to the top of a narrow trail above a rock outcrop that provided a natural overlook where they could view the rapids and determine if it was safe to pass. He explained if they decided it wasn't safe then the group would need to hike around the rapids while the boatman would navigate the raft down river alone and pick us up on the other side. When they hiked back down from the lookout and approached those of us sitting on the beach, someone in the group asked with a sense of anticipation what each of us was thinking; "How does it look? What do you think?"

"It's rough," the guide responded. "But I can position the raft above the rapid and follow a line of descent down, which I visualized in order to avoid a large hole to one side. I'd prefer to let you have the experience than make you hike around."

It was somewhat unnerving to hear him say that because we really thought he'd advise us to hike around. After all, the fact that the crew believed we needed to park the raft so they could inspect the rapid from above, seemed to warrant the seriousness of the danger. Otherwise, as an experienced boatman who had been through the canyon many times we assumed he'd just take us on through without stopping. So, the anxiousness we all felt by that time had grown.

* * *

It's hard to describe what happened when we hit that rapid fifteen minutes later. It seemed as if the river suddenly surged forward into a vortex, pulling us over the green colored face as it swallowed the entire raft that flexed mid-center as it bucked over the upper end before being pushed through by some unseen force. Everyone hung on for dear life as a wall of water exploded up and over the front of the raft completely soaking us. It was a rush that only lasted for a few glorious moments. And, we all made it! No one got swept overboard nor did the raft flip. The boatman obviously knew what he was doing, and he possessed both the skill and experience that enabled the group to enjoy the thrill. The incredible adrenaline-pumping feeling we all shared during those brief moments crashing through those rapids enabled us to feel that the entire four-day adventure was experienced at a level much deeper than it might have seemed had we walked around Granite Rapids. It counted for something truly epic and worthwhile.

* * *

The adventure on that river through Hells Canyon is the perfect metaphor of my missionary experience—and of life itself I suppose. Few stories are written with excitement about flat, calm rivers that meander slowly as the Snake River generally does as it passes by hundreds of miles of wildflower meadows and gently rolling sagebrush covered hills. The best stories are in the rapids, and that's where Krys and I have lived and worked for the past 25 years.

We often say that every day on the mission field is a new adventure and rarely does our work meander calmly for long distances. Throughout these many years, we've found ourselves symbolically navigating the team through rapids of all the various whitewater classifications, indicating a different level of difficulty. Sometimes the rapids had small waves and few obstructions that can be easily maneuvered around such as an embedded tree trunk or large rock. Other times presented ministry challenges equivalent to a Class V rapid where we needed to work our way through "long, obstructed, or violent rapids with drops that may contain large, unavoidable waves and holes or steep, congested chutes with complex demanding routes" as AW describes while advising people that "proper equipment, extensive experience, and practiced rescue skills are essential" for those classifications.

Prize winning author Emma Smith wrote; "Life is like the river, sometimes it sweeps you gently along and sometimes the rapids come out of nowhere." The crisis I endured at Outland came out of nowhere like a Class V rapid that pulled me in. At the time of this writing, it has been five years since I experienced the betrayal, and as I look in the rearview mirror I find it to be a fading blip on the radar screen of my missionary career. I chose to share the contours of that struggle in hopes it might help someone going through a realignment that might be, if they're willing to consider, "God-ordained" as Clinton wrote. If I had the chance to ride that particular rapid again, I would have responded differently in so many ways, but life has a habit of throwing stuff at us that is so unexpected it's impossible to prepare for a reaction, much less manage the crisis—like seeing a stick of dynamite suddenly appear in our lap.

*   *   *

The movie *Seabiscuit*, based on Laura Hillenbrand's best-selling book, is one of my favorites. Ironically, the main character is actually an overlooked and unfavorable Thoroughbred dismissed by several handlers because he was undersized and had knobby knees. A wealthy businessman by the name of Charles Howard acquired the colt and through a chance encounter meets an introverted drifter, Tom Smith, who happens to be a skilled horse trainer that quietly specializes in rehabilitating injured and abused horses. Howard ends up offering Smith a job who convinces Howard that Seabiscuit is worthy of some specialized attention, recognizing his potential to win more races. Previously, Seabiscuit lost 17 races, ending up near the back of the field. Smith slowly draws the colt out of its lethargy and it begins to show significant improvements, eventually winning races. However, the horse is not performing at the level Smith knows he's capable of winning, including the higher-level championship races. Every attempt Smith uses to get the horse to cut loose so the jockey can race him as a champion is met with continual disappointment. He finally says, "I can't help thinking he's forgotten what he was born to do. He just needs to learn how to be a horse again." Smith's unorthodox training method eventually pays off and Seabiscuit goes on to beat Triple Crown winner War Admiral in a race referred to as the "Match of the Century."

To borrow the analogy; I needed to be reinvented and let myself be taken back to a conversion experience where God could teach me "how to be a horse again." That conversion provided a more competent second look at my life as a missionary and created a new weakness in me that I've come to appreciate. Since that time, I have grown and matured in many ways. I'm far more sensitive to listen to God and pay attention to my wife. I can't say I'm a better missionary per se because there's no standard by which missionaries are determined to be good, but I do feel there's a new authenticity as a result of that weakness, and my approach to our ministry is much different than it had been all the previous years.

It was important that I communicated exactly that to the Filipino staff at the clinic, most of who had served for many years. When I turned my full attention back to the clinic I gathered the staff together in order to explain that I'd been an absent leader for several years and asked for their grace and forgiveness. It was important that my drive for a response from each one was prompted by a heart of genuine authenticity rather than just a pep talk from the boss. I'd gained a larger sense of responsibility for their personal employment and service to the ministry, and my goal was to be more than just a boss they were obligated to respect because I paid their salaries. I wanted to be a boss (*Amo*) they could fully trust to care for them as a shepherd does his sheep with their best interests at heart because, culturally, that is the type of relationship most Filipinos desire from their employers.

That understanding helped shape the significance of how I would serve as their boss in the future, which for me had become much more personal. However, I wasn't expecting the honesty of the responses I received afterward during private moments with a few employees who individually confided to me. One said they'd felt jealous of the attention I was giving to Outland, and another said they simply missed my presence at the clinic. Although I had often gone to the clinic each week, it was generally a quick walkthrough followed by a quick departure to head back to Outland. One comment that stood out above all others came from an employee who had spent almost 15 years with us, "We didn't only miss you. We needed you."

Three years later Krys and I faced an unexpected crisis after someone falsely fabricated a story against the ministry based on their personal prejudices, and laid an indictment at our feet that was extremely difficult to defend. The nature of the problem was much different than the false accusation I endured at Outland, but what I learned from that crisis helped Krys and I navigate this new storm. God is all-knowing, and had He not previously taken steps to realign me to serve the clinic in a full-time capacity it's possible we may have lost the ministry altogether. That crisis provided an added confirmation that God in His providence redirected my focus to where it needed to be.

* * *

In these pages I've attempted to share just a small portion of what we experienced during our time on the mission field, but even the stories surrounding the events cannot be expressed in sufficient detail to fully transfer the wealth of experiences at the level we lived them. John Eldredge wrote, "Life is not a problem to be solved, it is an adventure to be lived." A lot of personal growth and deepening of our relationship with Christ can be folded into the adventure that cross-cultural missions provide.

Krys recently reminded me of something I forgot when I asked her to marry me. Apparently, I promised to take her on an adventure if she was willing to be my wife. We left our home country 25 years ago to go to a foreign country steeped in grinding poverty, systemic corruption and socio-economic inequalities that victimize impoverished families. At the time of our initial arrival, when the wheels of the monstrous 747 plane touched down at the Manila airport, we held onto an escape clause inserted at the bottom of an abstract imaginary contract in which we committed to try it out for twelve months—at which time we could easily claim the "missions thing" didn't work for us if we decided that we didn't like it. Little did we know that God had other plans, which included turning that initial one-year "tryout" into decades in the land we now call home.

* * *

Cross-cultural missionary work has been referred to as the great theater of the Great Commission where people of tremendous capacity desire to serve the Lord, often enduring extremely difficult challenges. They have, to some degree, voluntarily given so much to serve as best they know how while struggling through so many adversities, yet continuing to move forward despite their failures and feelings of vulnerability. In my opinion Teddy Roosevelt's famous words resonate in the heart of every career missionary I know who has served several years on the field; "The credit belongs to the man who is actually in the arena, whose face is marred by dust and sweat and blood; who strives valiantly; who errs, who comes short again and again, because there is no effort without error and shortcoming; but who does actually strive to do the deeds; who knows great enthusiasms, the great devotions; who spends himself in a worthy cause; who at the best knows in the end the triumph of high achievement, and who at the worst, if he fails, at least fails while daring greatly, so that his place shall never be with those cold and timid souls who neither know victory nor defeat."

They aren't doing so by their own imagination, but by a deep sense of calling that only another missionary can identify with. People don't make precedents of how their missionary careers will endure, but rather, in their brokenness and struggles they strive to better understand how to make a difference by continually compromising their egos and surrendering to the conviction and leading of the Holy Spirit.

* * *

Since before we were married, Krys and I wanted to be a part of a story bigger than ourselves, and what better story to join than the global expansion of a 2,000-year-old narrative with a sprawling and ambitious history. The particular work we oversee is something we believe supports a viable strategic asset in helping to fulfill the Great Commission, despite how small it may seem in comparison to the totality of the World Christian Movement.

Krys and her Filipino national midwife team who work with us have trained and equipped more than 200 young ladies throughout these past many years. Our ministry mobilizes people to a foreign country within the context of the mission field itself; meaning we are on the receiving end, not as a mission sending agency. Primary of course is the midwifery program, but we also partner with other ministries such as Nehemiah Teams (NT), an organization that mobilizes U.S. college students to serve with national church planting teams. NT was founded by fellow missionaries, Jess and Wendy Jennings, who are close friends stationed in Davao City. To date, NT has mobilized students to over 60 unreached people groups in 30 different countries around the world working in remote villages and urban centers sharing the gospel. The Jennings recognize the validity a Christian midwife brings to the mission field and they have been very proactive in helping us train our students regarding cross-cultural missions by providing opportunities for them to participate with their church planting outreaches in the provinces of northern Mindanao.

Upon completion of our program, which is currently 2.5 years, many of our graduates return to their respective home countries in America, Canada and Europe to serve as Christian midwives. About 20% have gone on to serve as missionaries in countries that include Nigeria, Afghanistan, Nepal, India, China, Yemen, Sudan, Cambodia, Haiti, Solomon Islands, Chad, Sierra Leone, Mozambique, Congo, and Zambia. During this year alone we've seen two of our recent single graduates arrive in Chad-Zaire where they will serve as midwives with a large international mission organization. One of our married grads just arrived in Pakistan with her family where they plan to serve long term, also with a large mission organization. Another married lady who served in our intern program just arrived in Indonesia with her family to represent their denomination as overseas missionaries. And a third married graduate has been mobilized with her family to serve in Tanzania.

We've also sponsored the midwifery college education of several young ladies from the Philippine's Monobo Tribe in partnership with OMF (Overseas Missionary Fellowship). All but two of those young ladies returned to their tribal villages after completing their education and serving at our clinic for a two-year commitment, and two decided to stay long term at the clinic where they now serve as supervisors overseeing U.S. midwifery students.

In chapter fourteen I referenced a quotation from the book *Preach and Heal* regarding the tension between evangelism and social ministry. Our midwives are approaching the delivery of baby number 25,000 at our clinic as I write this, and I'll admit we're very sensitive not so much concerning the "tension" but the feeling of being responsible to follow up on those patients. The logistical challenge we face is the volume of patients who seek out our maternal healthcare services. I once heard a sermon in which the pastor said that Jesus, although God, was limited by time and distance. During His earthy ministry Jesus could only walk so many miles in a day and interact with so many people. It is physically impossible for us to follow up on 25,000 patients; not including the 25,000 additional patients who have come to the clinic for their prenatal exams but delivered their babies elsewhere or needed to be transported to the hospital due to complications requiring C-sections or other interventions the midwives are not allowed by law to manage.

* * *

Over the years God has blessed us with some incredible people who have served the team respective of their evangelistic gifting. Some students who excel relationally have done an exceptional job ministering to their patients and starting bible studies in their homes, while others are more introverted and not as comfortable going into someone's home to begin a bible study.

However, they're quite at ease praying for patients in the clinic during their check-ups. Various couples who have served with us over the years have also added tremendous value to the team regarding holistic ministry. Nolan and Salem Silvey stand out as an exceptional couple who helped develop our member support services, and they trained our foreign and national midwives to evangelize patients during follow up home visits. Their efforts went beyond simply developing a program because they were very intentional in encouraging our staff to be proactive in evangelism, and we've been careful to record the fruit of those efforts. As an example, during the past six months, as of this writing, 112 patients were visited in their homes where the gospel was shared 73 times. Personal testimonies of the midwives were shared 62 times. Sixteen patients accepted Christ and 43 asked to be visited again.

We often looked to the story Jesus shared about the Good Samaritan. He didn't lead the beaten man to Christ or invite him to a bible study or encourage him to join a church. He did, however, show compassion and helped the man to the best of his ability. We remain steadfast, believing the ministry of the midwives is fruitful in many regards as we show mercy and compassion to the broken, afraid and abused women who come to our clinic. Sometimes, however, fruit can appear to be elusive or remain hidden for many years, as happened with David and Svea Flood, Swedish missionaries who served in Belgian Congo in the early 1900s. Their story has been published and copied in countless books, articles, blogs and websites, and it's worth sharing once again so I'll provide a brief synopsis of this amazing true story.

David and Svea partnered with another couple, the Ericksons, planning to live among the people in a remote village, but the chief resisted. Both couples decided to erect mud huts a short distance from the village and prayed that God would provide a spiritual breakthrough. The villagers ostracized them, but allowed a young boy to sell them chicken eggs twice a week. Svea determined if the boy was the only person she could talk to then she would do her best to teach him about Jesus. Eventually the boy accepted Christ, but then tragedy struck. A bout of Malaria forced the Ericksons to return to the mission post, which left the Floods to continue the work alone.

Then, Svea became pregnant and after enduring a long and exhaustive labor she died several days after giving birth to a baby girl.

Overcome by grief, David Flood buried his wife in a crude grave then hiked down the mountain and handed his newborn daughter to the Ericksons and told them he was returning to Sweden. He exclaimed that God ruined his life and he rejected his calling as well as God himself. Eight months later, the Ericksons were stricken with a disease and died within days of each other. The baby girl was then given to an American missionary couple who decided to give her the Swedish name "Aggie" and ended up bringing her to America three years later.

Aggie grew up in South Dakota, then while attending Bible college in Minneapolis she married Dewey Hurst who several years later took a position as president of a Seattle Christian college where Aggie learned several of the students had a Scandinavian heritage.

One day a Swedish religious magazine appeared in her mailbox, which she couldn't explain. She couldn't understand the words, but as she flipped through the pages she saw a photo of a primitive grave with the name *SVEA FLOOD* written on the white cross erected at the head of the grave. Aggie found a faculty member she knew could translate the accompanying article, which he summarized for her. It was about missionaries who had come to a place called N'dolera long ago ... the birth of a white baby... the death of the young mother ... the one little African boy who had been led to Christ ... and how, after the whites had all left, the boy grew up and finally persuaded the chief to let him build a school in the village. The article said that gradually he won all of his students to Christ... the children led their parents to Christ... even the chief had become a Christian. Today there were six hundred Christian believers in that one village.... all because of the sacrifice of David and Svea Flood.

For the Hurst's twenty-fifth wedding anniversary, the college presented them with the gift of a vacation to Sweden where Aggie sought to find her real father. An old man now, David Flood had remarried, fathered four more children, and generally lived his life inside of a bottle of alcohol. He had recently suffered a stroke. After an emotional reunion with her half-brothers and half-sister, Aggie asked to see her father but was warned that he flew into a rage whenever he heard the name of God.

Aggie walked into the squalid apartment and told him that he didn't go to Africa in vain, and that her Mama didn't die for nothing. She explained, "The little boy you won to the Lord grew up to win that whole village to Jesus Christ. The one seed you planted just kept growing and growing. Today there are six hundred African people serving the Lord because you were faithful to the call of God in your life. ... Papa, Jesus loves you. He has never hated you." By the end of the afternoon he had come back to the God he once served so fervently. Aggie returned to America and within a few weeks, David Flood had gone into eternity.

A few years later, the Hursts were attending evangelism conference in London, England, when a report was given from Zaire (the former Belgian Congo). The superintendent of the national church, representing some 110,000 baptized believers, spoke eloquently of the gospel's spread in his nation. Aggie could not help but find him afterward and asked if he had ever heard of David and Svea Flood. "Yes, madam," the man replied in French, his words being translated into English. "It was Svea Flood who led me to Jesus Christ. I was the boy who brought food to your parents before you were born. In fact, to this day your mother's grave and her memory are honored by all of us." He embraced her in a long, sobbing embrace. Then he continued, "You must come to Africa to see, because your mother is the most famous person in our history." In time that is exactly what Aggie Hurst and her husband did. They were welcomed by cheering throngs of villagers. She even met the man her father had hired many years before to carry her back down the mountain in a hammock-cradle. The most dramatic moment, of course, was when the pastor escorted Aggie to see her mother's white cross for herself.

* * *

Wouldn't it be wonderful to see, many years from now, some resulting fruit of the seeds we planted—similar to what happened when Svea Flood shared the gospel with that little boy who sold her chicken eggs, but wasn't able to see that harvest this side of heaven. Throughout these many years, we've trained and equipped Philippine national pastors and lay leaders how to plant churches, and created an innovative avenue to reach thousands of youth for Christ who were deeply impacted not by a religious presentation, but by experiencing God in a way that was profoundly personal and intimate. We've also trained a small army of Christian midwives capable of transcending barriers to the gospel message as they are integrated and absorbed into communities in countries all over the world as "women of peace."

As Krys and I continue to move forward on the mission field, we may be privileged to learn that some of the Outland campers grew up to serve God as pastors, social workers, and business leaders in the community, school principals or teachers who strive to serve Christ and make a difference because their lives were transformed at one of our *Great Adventure Camps.* Perhaps we may read an article or a book many years from now narrating a story about one of Krys' graduates who joined a pioneering church planting team working with an unreached people group living on a distant island, barren desert, or mountainous jungle region who had never heard the gospel; and the key to gaining their favor came from the skills of a midwife — the midwife she spent two years training.

We witnessed a precursor of this several months ago while the two of us were sitting in a coffee shop at a local mall. We were approached by a young Filipino couple who introduced themselves as Ram and Janine and asked if I remembered them from 18 years ago. I did in fact remember spending time visiting them in the home of Janine's family. Her father ran a small taxi business near the apartment where Krys and I were living. They were single at the time, but engaged to be married; and were struggling to understand God's direction for their lives while studying at a bible school where I was teaching. Ram said that I had encouraged them to pursue the pastoral ministry because I had sensed God's calling on their lives to be pastors, a position they are now serving in after planting a new church in Tacloban City thirteen years ago, which has grown so large they are now meeting in a theater with 18 ministers on staff. Ram and Janine told me they would never have entered the ministry if it hadn't been for me, to which I replied that God would certainly have intervened regardless of my encouragement. But they were insistent that my influence was not going to be so easily dismissed, and they kept saying the time I had spent visiting with them over the course of a year or so was a pivotal point in their lives, which God used to direct them into ministry.

* * *

Maybe it's our human weakness and selfishness that causes us to measure achievements and successes by looking at milestones or ministries we've started or people we've influenced such as Ram and Janine. We value those achievements by their apparent significance and what they mean to us as a self-recognized personal accomplishment. However, even if the motive is right, that alone cannot be the incentive to serve and to sacrifice, regardless of where or how. What does matter is the role we're playing and the story God desires to tell through our lives that needs to count for something— something of eternal value.

Very early one morning several years ago, while I was sitting alone having my quiet time before the sun came up I expressed to God how difficult life was on the mission field; experiencing feelings of continual inadequacy. Trying to straddle two different worlds with differing values creates unique stresses that missionaries and expats encounter while living in a foreign culture, and as much as we try to assimilate and adapt, it can be incredibly arduous.

"Lord, this missionary life is hard," I said. "It's frustrating and challenging, and I miss my culture and my family back home."

Before ending my prayer, I said, "I just hope it all counts."

About three hours later I was down at the church with three other men who had gathered for a time of prayer and fellowship. We had known each other long enough to be comfortable being honest and somewhat vulnerable sharing prayer requests or talking about challenges we were enduring.

We were taking turns praying for each other, which meant that one of us was placed in the "prayer chair" while the other three concentrated their prayers for the one brother. A few minutes in, it was my turn to sit in the chair when one of the men, a Filipino elder in the church said, "Matt, I'm not sure if I have this right, but a phrase keeps coming to my mind as we're praying for you. I'm not sure what it means, but I feel God wants to tell you something."

I had known this brother for a few years and found him to be a godly man with a strong relationship with Christ. I also respected him very much, and a few years later God called him and his wife into full time ministry where he became a successful pastor whom God has continued to bless because of his humble heart.

I replied and said. "OK. If you feel God might have a word for me go ahead and tell me what it is."

He then said, "I feel that God just wants you to know it all counts."

I hope you enjoyed reading this book as much as I enjoyed writing it. Whether you loved it or didn't particularly care for it, I'd really appreciate your feedback. Feel free to leave your comments on Amazon.com or Goodreads.com.

Made in the USA
San Bernardino, CA
21 April 2017